GUITAR *signature licks*

GUITAR SOLOS
great of all time

by Wolf Marshall

ISBN 0-7935-9309-3

HAL•LEONARD®
CORPORATION

7777 W. BLUEMOUND RD. P.O. BOX 13819 MILWAUKEE, WI 53213

Visit Hal Leonard Online at
www.halleonard.com

greatest GUITAR SOLOS of all time

contents

INTRODUCTION

This special volume of *Guitar Signature Licks* is devoted to the art of the rock guitar solo. It is more than a mere collection of solos; it is the story of the evolution of the rock solo, as told musically by the greatest players in the genre, presented in a chronological progression spanning more than three decades. This volume itself was years in the making and offers more than a dozen of rock's greatest guitar soloists in career-defining musical moments. You'll see, hear, learn about, and experience the art from its humble rock 'n' roll roots to its modern innovations with eighteen classic guitar solos in a wide variety of styles. Signature licks, indeed.

—Wolf Marshall

PREFACE

The guitar solo in rock music is an aural tradition. Great soloists have learned the craft and musical lessons from their forefathers—absorbing the salient points (be it a Chuck Berry dyad, a B.B. King lick, or a tricky scalar run) and appropriating those which resonated most strongly for them. In the early stages, it is learned by listening, watching, assimilating, and imitating. Ultimately, the soloist embellishes upon those seminal ideas and stretches them to new, often unrecognizable, lengths to fashion their own unique creative statements. Much mystique and mystery surrounds the entire issue. Often the artist chooses to keep the matter an internal, subliminal phenomenon. Sometimes what goes on during the making of a solo is inexplicable—not because the soloist cannot explain their approach but because the process takes place (as it often must to be spontaneous) in the "world of non-thought." One goal of this signature licks volume is to fill in those gaps—to de-mystify the process and to present *useable* insights into the soloist's creative act. Another aim is to provide you with an environment to expound on the solo, after you have learned and mastered the crucial signature licks, via the accompanying audio portion.

In addition to valuable background information about the artist and the specific music in question, each selected solo contains a user-friendly, nutshell analysis—in effect, a "recipe" for the solo. This is a refinement of my teaching approach. The analysis addresses the essential points of scale usage, physical technique, and equipment. Furthermore, significant added tones are cited in the analysis to help you, the player, understand how a particular soloist incorporated melodic material outside the basic scale to color their musical statement. Performance notes are also included in the analysis section to specify and explain any unusual or explicit physical techniques and improvisational approaches. In order to properly place the analysis in a musical context, the scale(s) applied by the artist in the solo are marked by brackets in the score above the standard notation staff. This provides you with the understanding of what scale was selected to produce a particular sound—and where, when, and how it was used by the soloist. Through the acquisition of such information you will be in sync with the soloist's thinking and strategies. By learning, mastering, and absorbing the lessons in these solos you will place yourself in the tradition, and be well on your way to creating your own unique solo statements.

THE RECORDING

Wolf Marshall: guitars
Michael Della Gala: bass
Mike Sandberg: drums, percussion
John Nau: keyboards
Gary Ferguson: additional drums

The titles in this book include:

"Hound Dog"—Elvis Presley (with Scotty Moore)

"No Particular Place to Go"—Chuck Berry

"The Sunshine of Your Love"—Cream

"Hey Joe"—Jimi Hendrix

"While My Guitar Gently Weeps"—The Beatles (with Eric Clapton)

"The End"—The Beatles

"Babe I'm Gonna Leave You"—Led Zeppelin

"You Shook Me"—Led Zeppelin

"Evil Ways"—Santana

"Iron Man"—Black Sabbath

"All Right Now"—Free

"Bohemian Rhapsody"—Queen

"Walk this Way"—Aerosmith

"Sultans of Swing"—Dire Straits

"You Really Got Me"—Van Halen

"Crazy Train"—Ozzy Osbourne (with Randy Rhoads)

"Crossfire"—Stevie Ray Vaughan

"Sweet Child O' Mine"—Guns N' Roses

HOUND DOG
Words and Music by Jerry Leiber and Mike Stoller

Figure 1 – Guitar Solo

Scotty Moore is universally acknowledged as the world's first rock 'n' roll guitarist—a strong statement, perhaps…but consider this: His lead playing on Elvis Presley records in the 1950s set in motion, and brought to mass public attention, the art of rock guitar. Moore was the first rock guitar innovator. His style was truly eclectic and pioneering. Working without a preconceived blueprint, he freely combined elements from disparate influences such as country (Merle Travis and Chet Atkins), blues (B.B. King and T-Bone Walker), and jazz (Barney Kessell and Johnny Smith) to form the basis of his influential guitar approach. Before Scotty, rock 'n' roll guitar was an obscure and regional medium at best. With Scotty, rock 'n' roll guitar was codified and at the center of a revolution in popular music. Scotty blazed the trail for much of what followed, and inspired subsequent generations of rockers including the Beatles, the Stones, Jimmy Page, and countless others. His solos from the Sun Sessions and the early RCA years are deemed by most historians and legions of players to be the first of their kind—marking the beginnings of a vital new artform which still shows no signs of abating some 45 years later.

Scotty Moore's guitar solo on "Hound Dog," a raucous #1 hit single for the King in August, 1956, is one of his all-time best. The brief but memorable outing has many classic Moore signatures including swing-based, horn-like lines, rockabilly-flavored double-stop bends, and gritty blues-oriented string bending. It's played over one chorus of a 12-bar blues in C.

Scales used: C minor pentatonic (C–E♭–F–G–B♭); C major pentatonic (C–D–E–G–A); C Blues Scale (C–E♭–F–F♯–G–B♭).

Significant added tones: D♯ (measure 5); A (measures 6–11); B (measure 7).

Solo signatures: Mixture of single-note and dyad textures; double-stop bends; blues; country and swing phrasing within a rock 'n' roll context.

Performance notes: The single-note portions exploit a wider range of the guitar than had been previously found in most early rock 'n' roll single-note solos. These occur in the third, fifth, and eighth positions. Though Scotty Moore generally played with a thumbpick and three fingers, this sleek single-note solo sounds like he might be using only the thumbpick or a flatpick.

Sound: Gibson L-5 archtop hollowbody electric guitar with P-90 pickups and Gretsch heavy-gauge strings; small, slightly overdriven combo tube amps: Fender "TV-front" tweed Bassman or custom-made Echo-Sonic amp built by Ray Butts.

Featured Guitar:
(right Channel of audio)
Gtr. 1   meas.   1-13

Slow Demos:
Gtr. 1   meas. 1-3; 4-5;
6-9; 10-11; 12-13

Fig. 1

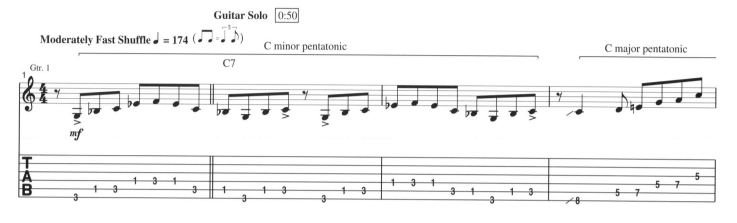

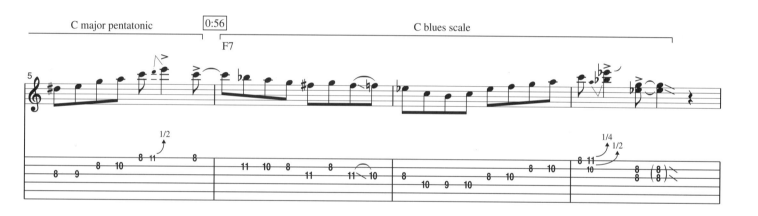

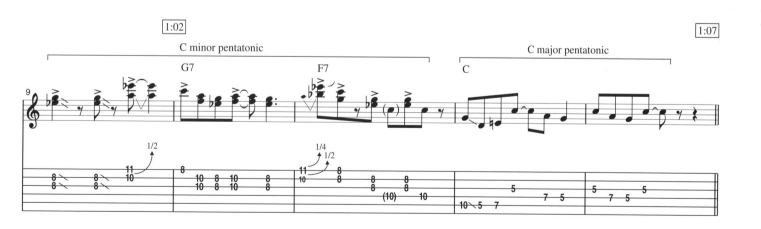

NO PARTICULAR PLACE TO GO

Words and Music by Chuck Berry

Figure 1 – Outro Guitar Solo

Chuck Berry is a true American icon and one of the most important founding fathers of rock guitar. Anyone picking up the instrument post-1955 has been affected by him, directly or indirectly, and that includes the Beatles, the Stones, Eric Clapton, Jimi Hendrix, Jimmy Page, Angus Young, Eddie Van Halen, Stevie Ray Vaughan, or the latest kid on the block. Chuck's own influences include blues guitarists Muddy Waters, T-Bone Walker, and Elmore James; R&B players Carl Hogan and Lonnie Johnson; jazz guitarists Charlie Christian and Django Reinhardt; and more esoteric musicians like saxophonist Illinois Jacquet. He once stated that he did not recognize any style of his own, though most historians regard his guitar style to be one of the single most significant factors in the development of rock music.

"No Particular Place to Go" is a case in point. This song was one of Chuck's biggest hits (#10 in 1964) and remains an immortal piece of the rock guitar legacy—containing a must-know guitar solo in the outro. The outro solo takes place over two choruses of a 12-bar blues in G, and exploits the trademark rhythm-lead approach which exemplifies the Chuck Berry solo style.

Scales used: G Mixolydian mode (G–A–B–C–D–E–F); G Blues Scale (G–B♭–C–D♭–D–F).

Significant added tones: E♭—used as a passing tone in the blues cadence of the last two measures.

Solo signatures: Shuffle-based blues feel; slurred triads and bent double stops; scales and modes freely combined, harmonized in parallel double stops, and played rhythmically.

Performance notes: The solo is almost entirely chordal, alternating between triad and dyad textures. Chuck plays many of these chordal sounds as thematic riffs. He introduces an idea and then develops it by repetition in the following measures—as in measures 4–5, 6–9, 13–15, or 18–19. During more aggressive dyad riffs, Berry strums the figures and mutes out extraneous unwanted notes with the frethand. The solo is situated in the "barre-chord" boxes (minor pentatonic pattern 1) in G at the fifteenth and third positions.

Sound: Gibson ES-355 or ES-345 with two humbucking pickups and vibrola tailpiece; slightly overdriven Fender combo tube amps and Fender Dual Showman piggyback amps.

Fig. 1

1:53

Moderate Rock ♩ = 132 (♫ = ♪ ♪)

Outro Guitar Solo

Gtr. 2: w/ Rhy. Fig. 1

G

9

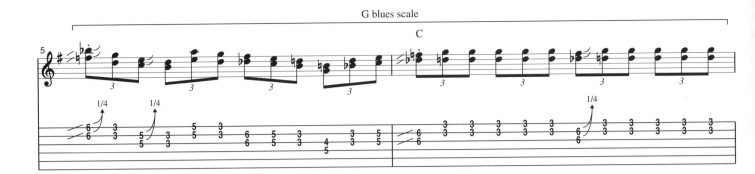

G blues scale

C

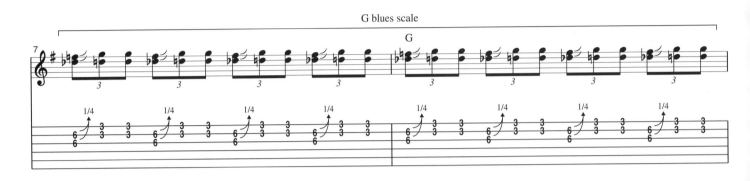

G blues scale

G

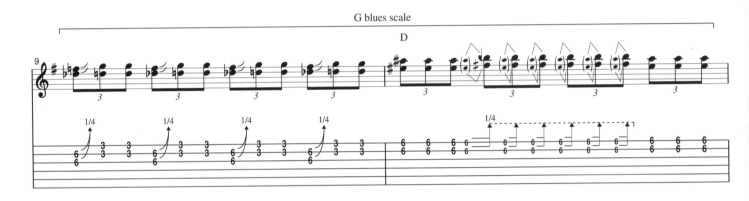

G blues scale

D

G blues scale

G Mixolydian mode

C

G

2:16

G Mixolydian mode

Gtr. 2: w/ Rhy. Fig. 1, 1st 10 meas.

G

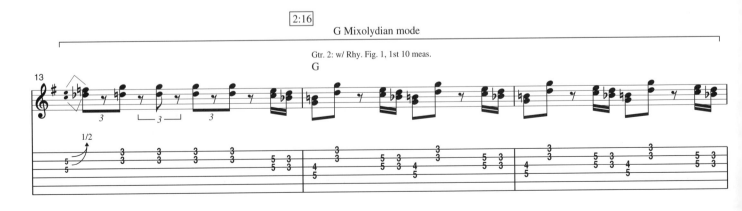

SUNSHINE OF YOUR LOVE

Words and Music by Jack Bruce, Pete Brown, and Eric Clapton

Figure 1 – Guitar Solo

Eric Clapton was rock's first guitar virtuoso. With Cream, rock's first power trio, Clapton set the tone and attitude for electric guitar soloing in the sixties and beyond. His fusion of Chicago and Texas blues with British hard rock marked a new direction in modern music and remains the standard by which most rock solos are judged. Eric's groundbreaking efforts with Cream laid the foundation for the incipient genres of hard rock and metal, as in the Jimi Hendrix Experience, Led Zeppelin, Black Sabbath, and other bands too numerous to name. His influence was enormous and pervasive. Hendrix refused to emigrate to England until he was promised he would meet Clapton, and even futuristic jazz guitarist Allan Holdsworth cites Eric as a seminal influence, as do contemporary virtuosi Eddie Van Halen and Eric Johnson.

"Sunshine of Your Love" was unarguably Cream's biggest hit—#5 in 1968. Recorded in 1967, the song contains Clapton's most well-known solo of the era—which is saying a lot. Played over an expanded, twenty-four-measure "altered blues progression" in D, the signature rock solo features many of his most unmistakable traits. Clapton's main influences as an electric guitar soloist included the Kings (B.B., Albert, and Freddie), Otis Rush, and Buddy Guy. Many of these influences are heard, often in mutated form, during the course of the "Sunshine of Your Love" solo.

Scales used: D minor pentatonic (D–F–G–A–C); D major pentatonic (D–E–F♯–A–B).

Significant added tones: B (measure 2); G♯ (measures 6 and 8).

Solo signatures: Major and minor scale combining; wide string bending and vibrato; use of amp sustain and overdrive distortion to create a vocal sound.

Performance notes: This classic solo is a virtual textbook of Clapton guitar moves. The blues-based wide string bends and vibrato (as in the major third bends of measure 10) require considerable hand strength and are best performed with reinforced fingering (more than one finger pushing the string)—a very visible Clapton technique. The pre-bends and held bends in measures 4 and 5, as well as the double-stop bends in measures 6 and 8, similarly benefit from reinforced fingering. The solo is situated in blues-box positions in D at the seventh, tenth, and twelfth frets (patterns 5, 1, and 2).

Sound: Gibson SG/Les Paul Standard with two humbucking pickups; overdriven 100-watt Marshall stacks with 4x12 cabinets.

7 Featured Guitars:
Gtr. 1 meas. 1-2
Gtr. 2 meas. 2-26
Gtr. 2 meas. 27-30

8 Slow Demos:
Gtr. 2 meas. 2-9;
10-15; 16-21;
22-27

Fig. 1

1:57

Moderate Rock ♩ = 112

Guitar Solo 2:01

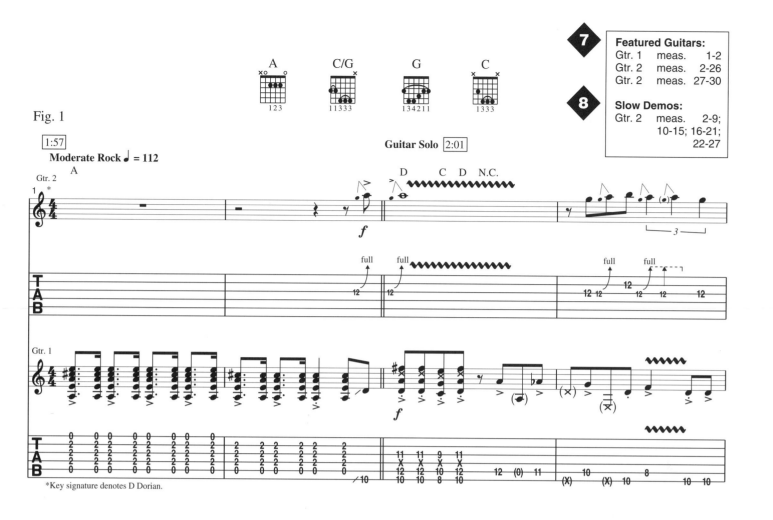

*Key signature denotes D Dorian.

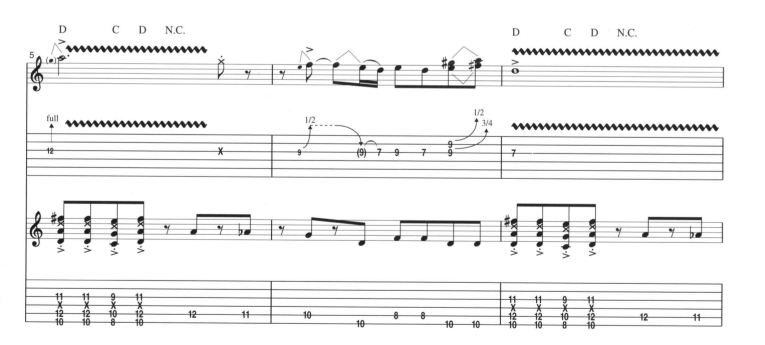

HEY JOE
Words and Music by Billy Roberts

Figure 1 – Guitar Solo

Jimi Hendrix is rock's ultimate guitar hero. He effectively moved rock guitar from the electrified blues genre of the sixties into uncharted regions of the 21st century—and we still haven't caught up with him! An intensely creative and multi-faceted player, Jimi was brought up on blues and R&B—favorites included Howlin' Wolf, Muddy Waters, B.B. and Albert King, Elmore James, and Buddy Guy as well as Curtis Mayfield and James Brown. He combined and transformed a wide array of influences as both a musician and composer to produce a powerful legacy of sounds and techniques not equalled or surpassed to the present day.

"Hey Joe" was Jimi's first hit and interestingly was not his original composition. In fact, the Billy Roberts tune received multiple covers in the mid-sixties (even one by Cher) before Hendrix touched it. However, once Jimi made it his debut single in 1967, he owned it. From then on, his was the definitive version. The song became a vehicle for Jimi's patented lead-rhythm comping approach and the perfect setting for one of his famous guitar solos.

In contrast to most of the extended, psychedelic rave-up improvisations of his career, this signature eight-measure Hendrix solo is brief, economical, and highly accessible. It occurs over two cycles of the tune's C–G–D–A–E verse changes, and culminates in a walking ensemble line with the bass for a funky R&B finish.

Scales used: E minor pentatonic (E–G–A–B–D).

Significant added tones: C♯ and F♯ (measure 8).

Solo signatures: Blues melody, feel, and phrasing despite non-blues musical environment; string bending and vibrato; double stops (measure 6); interval jumps of a sixth and a fourth in the minor pentatonic scale (measure 6).

Performance notes: Jimi's solo is primarily situated in the twelfth position E blues box. Reinforced fingering is used for the string bends and henceforth—due in great part to Hendrix's influence—became a norm in rock guitar solos. The double stops in measure 6 indicate the presence of Jimi's chord-melody conception in largely single-note solos.

Sound: Fender Stratocaster; slightly overdriven 100-watt Marshall stacks.

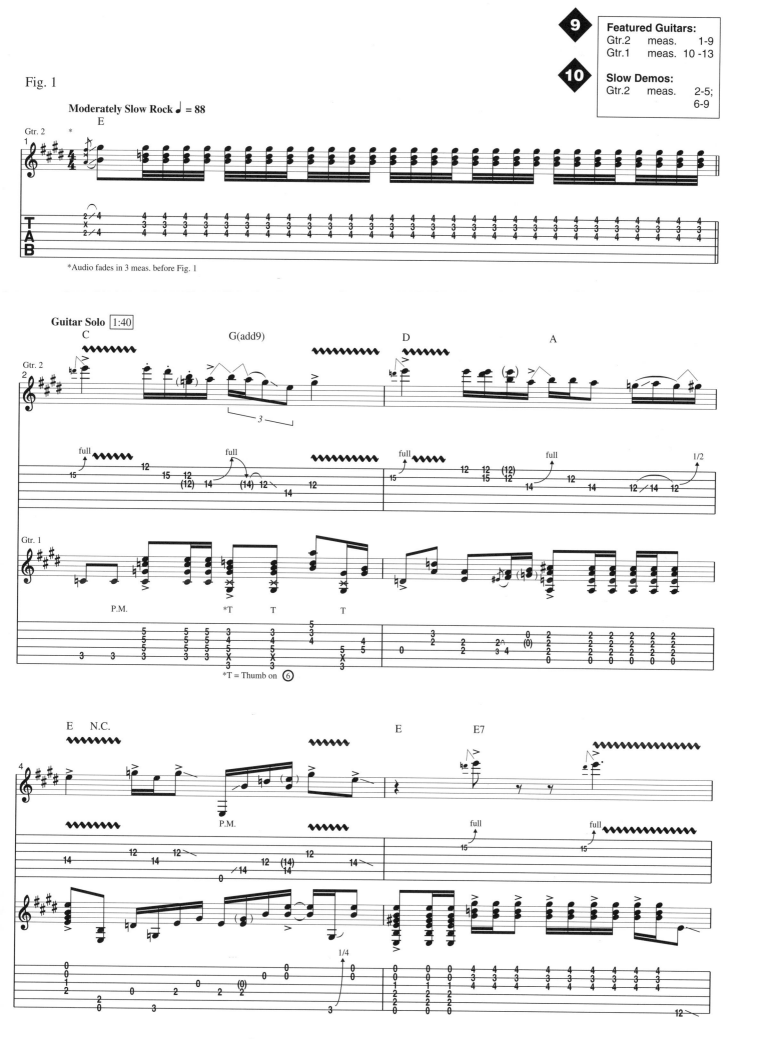

Fig. 1

*Audio fades in 3 meas. before Fig. 1

*T = Thumb on ⑥

WHILE MY GUITAR GENTLY WEEPS

Words and Music by George Harrison

Figure 1 – Guitar Solo

This classic cut from the Beatles' *White Album* of 1968 is distinguished by one of the most notable guest spots in rock history. At composer George Harrison's insistence, British blues-rock virtuoso Eric Clapton sat in with the world's biggest and most important band, a first, on the landmark track "While My Guitar Gently Weeps." Eric had done a number of sessions prior to the date (Aretha Franklin, Otis Spann, Champion Jack Dupree, Jackie Lomax, Martha Velez), but this proved to be a career high point. The momentous solo was recorded during a Beatle session on September 6, 1968, at Abbey Road Studios in London.

Eric Clapton's eight-measure contribution suits the tune perfectly—in both a melodic and thematic sense. Over the song's mixed-mode chord changes in A minor, Eric produces one of his most emotional and well-crafted signature solos of all time. The climax phrase in the last measure contains an ascending run in a faster sixteenth rhythm which would become a recurring concept in many future rock solos.

Scales used: A minor pentatonic (A–C–D–E–G).

Significant added tones: B and C♯ (pickup measure); E♭ (measure 6); all as a result of string bends.

Solo signatures: Blues melody and vocal guitar phrasing within a non-blues context; wide string bends and vibrato; compositional structure.

Performance notes: This Clapton solo is based entirely on the A minor pentatonic scale and is played almost exclusively in the twelfth position. Rather than motion, the focus is on emotion—string bends of practically infinite variety to emphasize the weeping theme of the composition. Of these, note particularly the pre-bends in the pickup and measures 4–6, and the wide string bending and wide vibrato in measures 3–6. The wide bends of a minor third (A to C) are slowly released while vibratoed for a particularly expressive crying effect.

Sound: Gibson Les Paul Standard; overdriven Marshall amp; ADT (Automatic Double Tracking, a studio chorusing effect) added to the guitar solo after it was recorded.

Fig. 1

11 Featured Guitar:
Gtr. 2   meas.   1-17

12 Slow Demos:
Gtr. 2   meas.   1-17

Guitar Solo

1:53

Slowly ♩ = 58

20

THE END

Words and Music by John Lennon and Paul McCartney

Figure 1 – Chorus and Guitar Solos

Abbey Road (1969) marked the last musical moments of the Beatles' illustrious career. The album's final moments, appropriately titled "The End," featured an auspicious solo in which all three guitar-wielding players traded back-to-back signature licks. By this point, the role and concept of the "Beatles lead guitarist" was completely blurred. Paul McCartney, George Harrison, and John Lennon equally and routinely handled solos on the band's various tracks as the situation arose.

In "The End," Paul, George, and John (in that running order) play off each other in a spirited guitar trio, and present us with an ideal opportunity to examine their individual lead styles. The solo takes place over a vamp of A7 to D7—somewhat like the first two measures of a blues progression in A. Each player handles his two-measure spot differently and assumes a contrasting guitar tone.

Scales used: All three soloists—A minor pentatonic (A–C–D–E–G); A Blues Scale (A–C–D–D♯–E–G).

Significant added tones: D♯ (measure 27) and C♯ (measure 31), both as a result of string bends; B (measure 32); F♯ (measures 44–45).

Solo signatures: Paul—semi-clean guitar tone, with an emphasis on rhythmic elements; George—semi-distorted tone and a Claptonesque blues-rock approach; John—distorted tone with the use of triads and low-register lines.

Performance notes: Paul's single-note lines are choppy and angular, emphasizing syncopation and eccentric phrasing. His tone is the cleanest and brightest. George's licks are smooth and melodious, reminiscent of Eric Clapton's style of the period with a slower, singing vibrato and blues-based string bending. Note the signature sliding line in measure 42. It's similarity to Clapton's closing phrase in "While My Guitar Gently Weeps" is inescapable. George's lines are delivered with a warmly distorted, midrangey sound. John's lead work is angry and punkish. His tone has the most distortion and a very thick, bassy timbre.

Sound: Paul—most likely Fender Esquire; George—probably the same Gibson Les Paul Standard used by Clapton for "While My Guitar Gently Weeps"; John—Epiphone Casino with overdriven Fender Twin-Reverb amps.

Fig. 1

Featured Guitars:
Gtr. 1   meas. 1-10
Gtr. 1   meas. 19-28
Gtrs. 2-4 meas. 28-47

Slow Demos:
Gtrs. 2-4 meas. 29-47

23

Chorus

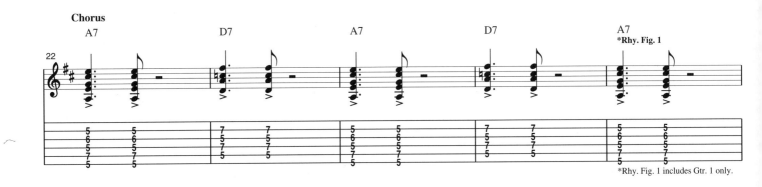

*Rhy. Fig. 1 includes Gtr. 1 only.

Guitar Solo 0:54

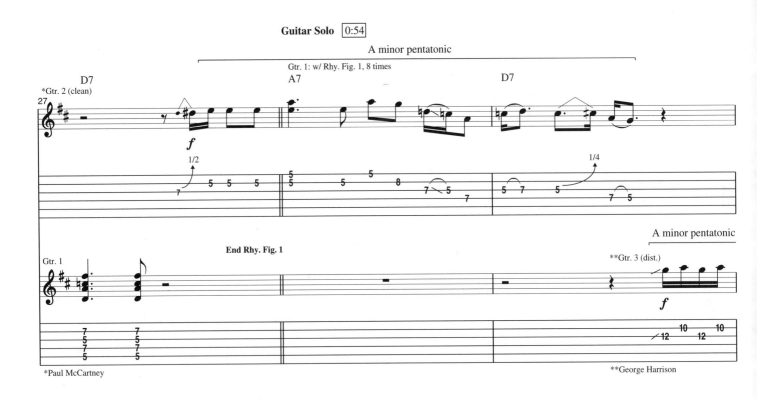

*Paul McCartney

**George Harrison

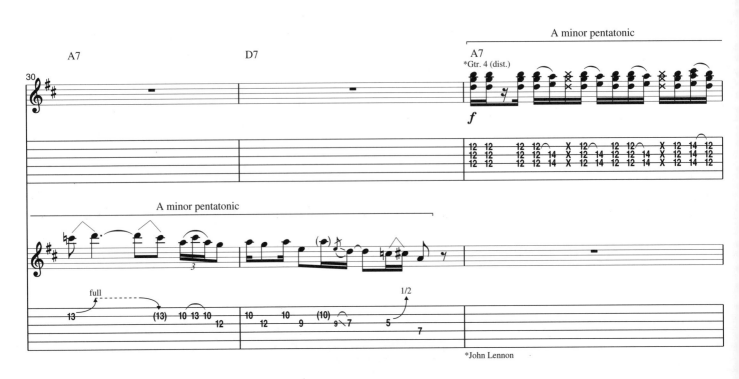

*John Lennon

*This measure played simile on demo

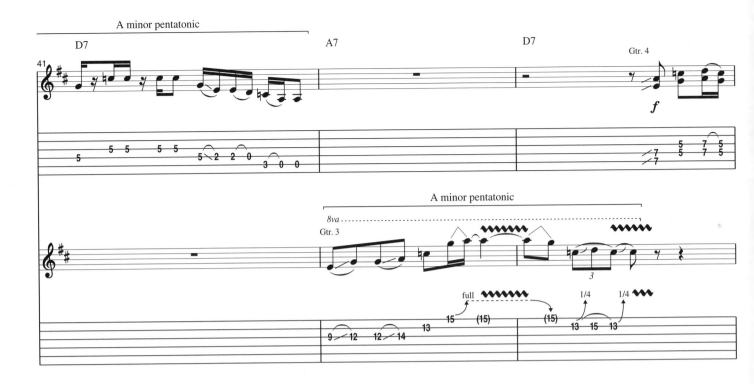

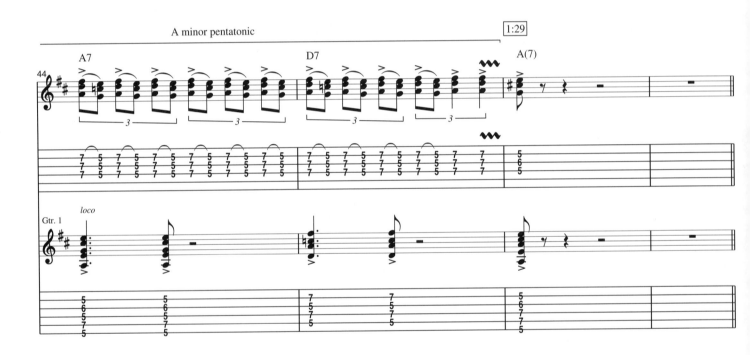

BABE, I'M GONNA LEAVE YOU

Words and Music by Anne Bredon, Jimmy Page, and Robert Plant

Figure 1 – Guitar Solo

Jimmy Page, a veteran of the mid-sixties rock session scene in London as well as a crony of Eric Clapton and Jeff Beck in the late-sixties British blues explosion, joined the legendary Yardbirds in 1966 and inherited the legacy by 1968. From those ashes rose first the New Yardbirds and finally Led Zeppelin in 1969. Page brought to bear all his session savvy as a composer, arranger, and musician on the groundbreaking debut album *Led Zeppelin.* The proof of the pudding is in tracks like "Babe I'm Gonna Leave You." This prototype power ballad set strong precedents for both the genre of hard rock/metal and the future direction of the mighty quartet's music. Balancing light acoustic and hard-rock timbres, it presented the world with an early view of Zep's trademark use of terraced dynamics, and Jimmy Page's well-conceived guitar orchestration.

For the solo in "Babe I'm Gonna Leave You," Jimmy Page chose to play steel-string acoustic guitar. He takes his compelling twenty-measure ride over a mixed-mode vamp in A minor—basically a variation of the verse chord progression played by the song's primary acoustic guitar.

Scales used: A Dorian mode (A–B–C–D–E–F♯–G); A Natural Minor or Aeolian mode (A–B–C–D–E–F–G); A Blues Scale (A–C–D–D♯–E–G).

Significant added tones: B (measure 10).

Solo signatures: Modal scalar lines mixed with blues bends and blues-rock phrasing; thematic development.

Performance notes: This acoustic guitar solo is purely in single notes and played with a flat pick. Page uses the full range of the acoustic guitar, moving through multiple position changes and exploiting open-string, first-position licks in measures 10–13. The gypsy-inspired diatonic lines (measures 2–5 and 16–17) contrast nicely with the blues bends in measure 6 and 7 and the blues slurs in measures 10–12. The raked seventh-chord arpeggios in measures 14–15 are a strong climax riff phrase, rhythmically and melodically. They are based on superimposed Em7 shapes played against the A minor tonal center, and produce a jazzy, extended-chord (Am11) effect.

Sound: Miked steel-string acoustic—most likely the borrowed Gibson J-200 that Page has cited as used on the sessions.

Featured Guitar:
Gtr. 3   1-20

Slow Demos:
Gtr. 3 meas. 2-3; 4-5;
6-9; 10-13; 14-17;

Fig. 1

Guitar Solo [4:50]
Moderate Rock ♩ = 134

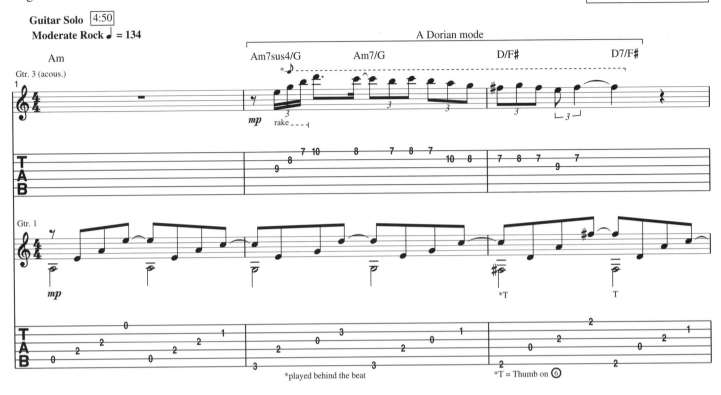

*played behind the beat   *T = Thumb on ⑥

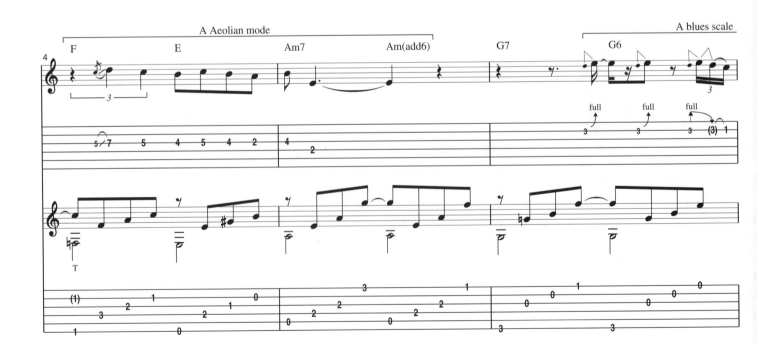

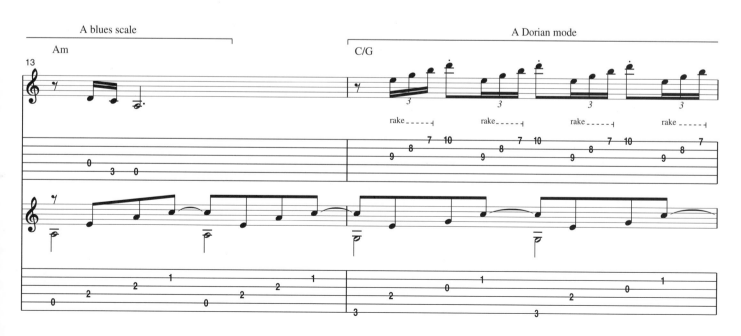

YOU SHOOK ME
Written by Willie Dixon and J. B. Lenoir

Figure 1 – Guitar Solo

"You Shook Me" exemplifies the electric side of Jimmy Page on the Zeppelin debut album. Page's transformation of Muddy Waters's Chicago blues standard into heavy metal on the first Zep album is a legendary moment in rock history, establishing an important and influential "fusion music" with powerful future implications. Page's guitar influences include proto-rockers Scotty Moore, Chuck Berry, blues players Muddy Waters, the Kings (B.B., Albert, and Freddie), Elmore James, and blues-rock contemporaries Eric Clapton and Jeff Beck. He has gone on to influence generations of rock players with his unique electric guitar style.

Jimmy Page's "You Shook Me" solo occurs over a slow 12-bar blues in E. His approach bridges the gap between updated Chicago blues, sixties blues-rock, and early heavy metal.

Scales used: E Mixolydian mode (E–F♯–G♯–A–B–C♯–D); E minor pentatonic (E–G–A–B–D); E major pentatonic (E–F♯–G♯–B–C♯).

Significant added tones: B♭ (measures 7–8, 13).

Solo signatures: Slide and standard guitar; modal melody (measures 3–6); minor and major scale combining; blues-oriented string bending and vibrato; double-timed riff flurries of sixteenth notes in measures 7–9.

Performance notes: Page plays slide in standard tuning during the first third of the solo (measures 3–6), employing a combination of bottle-neck and fingered technique. The remainder of the solo is done without the slide. The multi-note lines in measures 7–9 are played in the seventeenth position ("B.B. Box") and make use of mixed E minor and major pentatonic scales. Aggressive lines like these would have a profound effect on future guitar soloists in rock and metal. The final four measures are situated in standard blues box positions in E at the twelfth and ninth/eighth frets.

Sound: Fender Telecaster; overdriven Supro combo with a single 12" speaker—according to Page "all of the first album was done on that" (using that guitar/amp combination); chrome metal slide; harmonizer, reverb, and echo are discernable in spots, probably added in the studio.

Gtr. 1: w/ Rhy. Fill 1 (see next page)

Rhy. Fill 1

Gtr. 1

EVIL WAYS

Words and Music by Sonny Henry

Figure 1 – Outro Guitar Solo

As the sixties came to a close, a new era of guitar experimentation loomed in the future. While British bands like Led Zeppelin and Black Sabbath pushed forward the frontiers of blues-rock with metal, a stateside band from San Francisco named after its innovative lead guitarist presented their own brand of fusion music. Santana came to prominence in 1969, after a captivating appearance at Woodstock, national exposure on the Ed Sullivan Show, and the release of their remarkable debut record *Santana.* "Evil Ways" was a stand-out track on the album—a showcase number which succinctly captured the unique Latin/rock/jazz/blues amalgam of the Santana band and Carlos Santana's sophisticated lead guitar style.

Carlos's "Evil Ways" guitar solo is played over an animated version of the Gm–C7 vamp (like a repeating ii–V progression) heard in the verse. Santana's guitar influences include blues (B.B. King, Muddy Waters, and Otis Rush), jazz (Wes Montgomery, Gabor Szabo, and Bola Sete), and rock (Jimi Hendrix, Mike Bloomfield, and Eric Clapton). He blends them all beautifully in the song's memorable ride-out solo.

> **Scales used:** G Dorian mode (G–A–B♭–C–D–E–F); G minor pentatonic (G–B♭–C–D–F).
>
> **Significant added tones:** A and E, used throughout—though not strictly non-harmonic or chromatic added tones (they are diatonic to the Dorian mode), their deliberate use creates specific jazz-oriented extensions (ninth and thirteenth) which are at the heart of Santana's solo style.
>
> **Solo signatures:** Alternation between modal diatonic lines and blues licks. Syncopation and rhythmic devices used as themes. Rhythmic ostinato riffs (measures 14–16, 16 and 17, 20 and 21). Accelerating rhythm (measures 20 and 21). Use of amp distortion and sustain.
>
> **Performance notes:** Carlos exploits the full range of the fretboard, gravitating to the box positions of G minor pentatonic for blues licks as in measures 13 and 25–30. Most of his modal lines are played on one or two strings in a given phrase and are based on short repeated motifs rather than long scalar runs. The unison bends in the final measures are held and picked.
>
> **Sound:** Gibson SG Special; overdriven Fender Twin Reverb.

Fig. 1

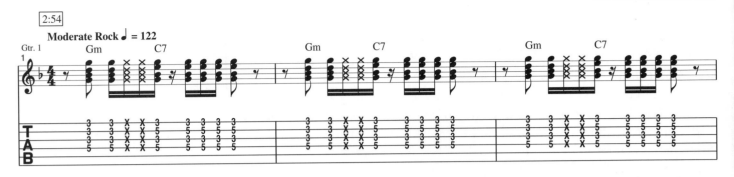

*Chords implied by organ and bass.

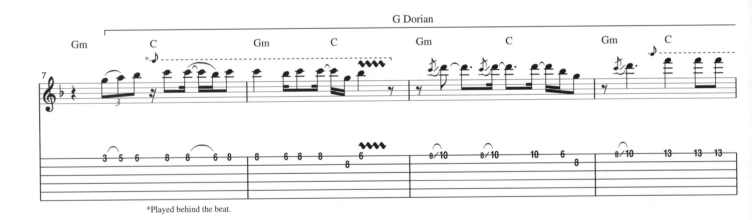

*Played behind the beat.

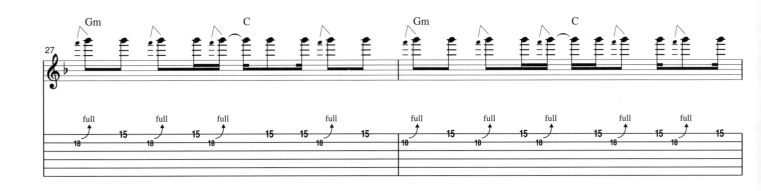

3:56

Repeat and Fade

IRON MAN

Words and Music by Frank Iommi, John Osbourne, William Ward, and Terence Butler

Figure 1 – Guitar Solo

Black Sabbath personified the dark, dungeonistic side of heavy metal in the seventies. With vivid horror-film mythology and gothic themes, they explored new levels of heaviness—lyrically and sonically. Underneath the lofty theatrics and black-magic trappings, Tony Iommi was a straightforward hard rock and electric-blues guitarist, a logical descendant of the Eric Clapton-Jimmy Page school of the late sixties. Iommi's guitar work with Sabbath set undeniable precedents for late-seventies metal, as well as the thrash style of the eighties and the heavier alternative sounds of the nineties. His solo in the early heavy metal classic "Iron Man" from the landmark Black Sabbath *Paranoid* album is an early milestone and a career high point— frequently cited by today's metal and hard rock guitarists as a strong influence.

Tony Iommi's "Iron Man" solo is played over one chord or tonal area (C♯ minor) implied by the bass and the solo guitar melody. The solo is in a charging double-time feel which alludes to Cream-era Eric Clapton—a major influence in Tony's style. The solo is introduced with a single-note ensemble riff in C♯ minor (measures 1–4) which is restated at the end of the solo in measures 21–24.

Scales used: C♯ minor pentatonic (C♯–E–F♯–G♯–B)

Significant added tones: G (measures 10 and 14) as a result of string bending.

Solo signatures: Riff-based soloing balanced with free pentatonic scale playing; prevalent use of hammer-ons and pull-offs; almost continuous eighth-note rhythm, with sixteenth-note ornaments.

Performance notes: Tony's solo is situated predominately in two minor pentatonic boxes—C♯ minor pentatonic at the fourth position and the ninth position. Theme riffs are played in measures 6–7 and 15–16. Iommi uses a repeated, hammered-on C♯ note in measures 17–20 as a signal riff to "conduct" the band's return to the song.

Sound: Gibson SG; overdriven Marshall stacks; modified Rangemaster treble booster for gain boost.

Fig. 1

Moderately Slow Rock ♩ = 76
Double-Time Feel

N.C.(C♯m)

*Audio fades in 4 meas. before Fig. 10.

Guitar Solo

(C♯m)

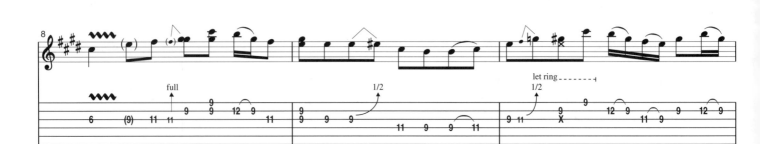

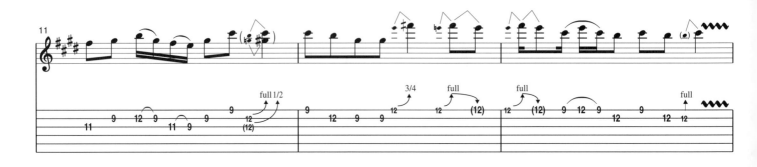

ALL RIGHT NOW
Words and Music by Paul Rodgers and Andy Fraser

Figure 1 – Guitar Solo

Paul Kossoff came to prominence in the early seventies with the British hard rock band Free. When the group scored big in 1970 with the smash single "All Right Now," Kossoff emerged from relative obscurity to international stardom practically overnight. Kossoff's blues-based rock style, with its emphasis on string bending, singing vibrato, and mutated blues licks, has much in common with late-sixties Eric Clapton—which is hardly a surprise considering that they employed similar instruments and shared many common seminal blues guitar influences such as B.B. and Freddie King.

Paul Kossoff recalled that his lead guitar work on "All Right Now" was added last—after the bass, piano, and rhythm guitar—and that necessitated that his playing be simple. Nonetheless, Kossoff's solo is a true seventies signature rock guitar solo and fits the song like a glove. It is played in two sections: the first is essentially an extended break without a definite chordal accompaniment; the second—beginning in measure 13—occurs over a two-measure vamp of G–D/F♯–A. This section builds in momentum until a strong climax is reached in the final measures.

Scales used: A minor pentatonic (A–C–D–E–G); A major pentatonic (A–B–C♯–E–F♯).

Significant added tones: C♯ (measures 2 and 6) as a result of string bends; C (measure 22); F♯ (measure 44).

Solo signatures: Blues-based string bends and vibrato; use of open strings in solo.

Performance notes: Kossoff responds to the larger, sectional nature of the solo by strategically alternating moods, ideas, and changing the register of his playing. Measures 1–8 are comprised of jabbing minor pentatonic blues licks in the thirteenth position. The beginning of the second section is laid back and sparse with long notes in the lower register. These are slurred and sustained with vibrato. The melodies in measures 14–35 are based by contrast on major pentatonic sounds. From measure 24 on, Paul plays in the upper register. The riffs in measures 25, 28, 36, and 40 are thematically repeated, and are played in first major, and then minor, pentatonic form.

Sound: Gibson Les Paul Standard; overdriven Marshall 100-watt stack.

Featured Guitar:
Gtr. 1   meas. 1–46

Slow Demos:
Gtr. 1   meas. 1–8;
          13–45

Fig. 1

Guitar Solo

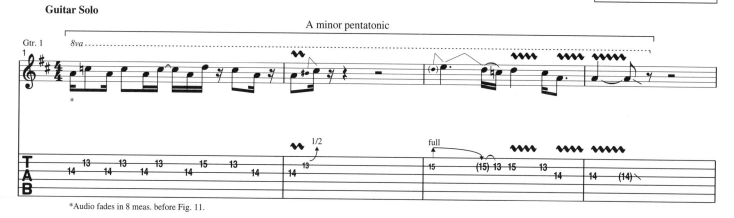

*Audio fades in 8 meas. before Fig. 11.

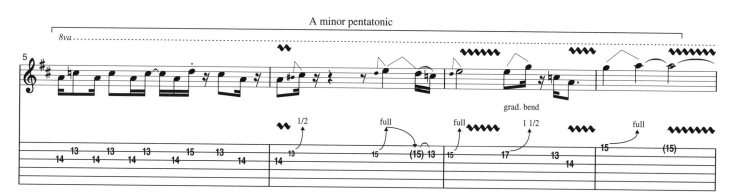

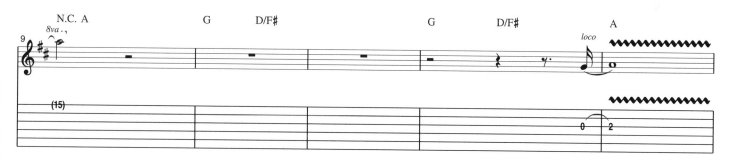

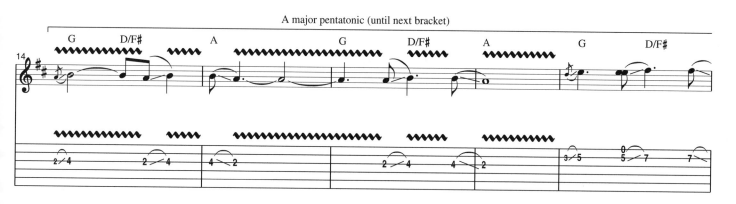

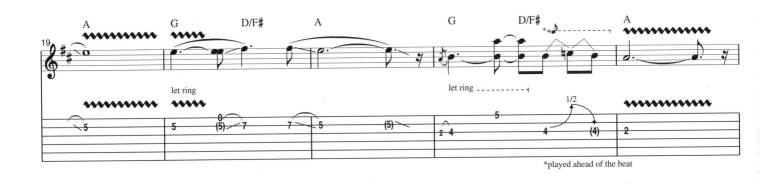

*played ahead of the beat

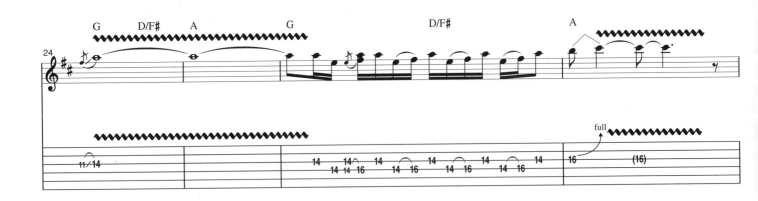

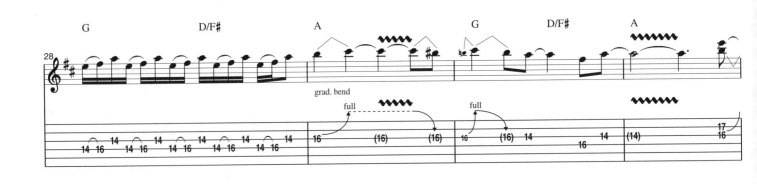

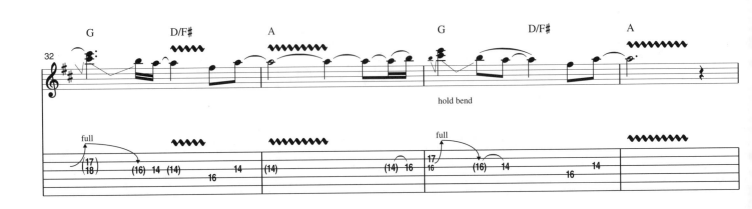

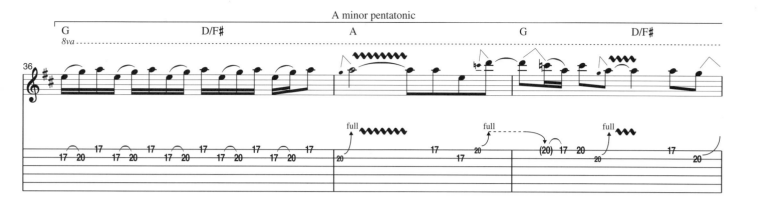

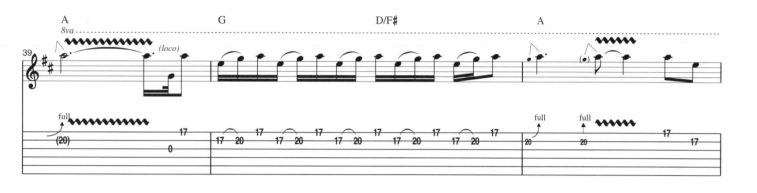

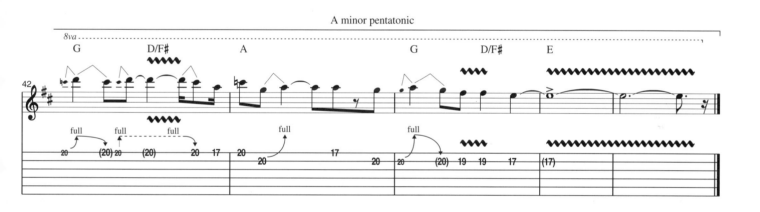

BOHEMIAN RHAPSODY

featured in the Motion Picture *WAYNE'S WORLD*

Words and Music by Freddie Murcury

Figure 1 – Guitar Solo

Queen was one of the few bands in rock history to enjoy both commercial success and artistic freedom. Their music—distinctly British and very regal—combined the eclectic experiments of the Beatles and the aristocratic quirkiness of English progressive rock bands like Yes with the larger-than-life heaviness of Led Zeppelin. "Bohemian Rhapsody" was Queen's coup. The crowning track of their masterpiece album, 1975's *A Night at the Opera,* it remains a gigantic global hit and an indispensable piece in the annals of classic rock. A complex and sprawling six-minute-plus epic, it is distinguished by state-of-the-art arranging and production, superb musicianship, and one of the most memorable and melodic guitar solos in the rock genre.

Brian May's eight-measure solo in "Bohemian Rhapsody" is definitive. Clearly ahead of its time, it blends melodic elements of classical music with the sonics of hard rock—anticipating a medium and trend which came to much greater prominence in the late seventies and eighties.

Scales used: E♭ major (E♭–F–G–A♭–B♭–C–D).

Significant added tones: D♭—used during the modulation in measure 8.

Solo signatures: Composed style; stately semi-classical phrasing; strong note-to-chord relationship in the melody; mixture of slow, lyrical lines and faster, scalar playing.

Performance notes: This classic Brian May solo is based on diatonic scalar lines in E♭ major, an unusual key for rock. The basic major scale is used modally throughout to create lines for specific chords in the progression, as in measures 3–4, where it is used against Fm and B♭7 chords. Ornamental trills are added to the ladder-like sequence melody in measure 4. Pure scalar runs are used in measure 5. Brian May employed a coin (English sixpence) with a serrated edge as a pick for his very strong, accented attack. This attack, coupled with the saturated tube-amp tone and signal processing, creates semi-harmonics throughout the solo.

Sound: Homemade "Red Fireplace" guitar with three reworked Burns single-coil pickups; overdriven Vox AC-30 amps; homemade treble booster; custom pre-amp built by Queen bassist John Deacon; flanging/chorusing added to thicken the guitar sound.

Fig. 1

Featured Guitar:
Gtr. 3   meas. 1-9

Slow Demos:
Gtr. 3   meas. 1-8

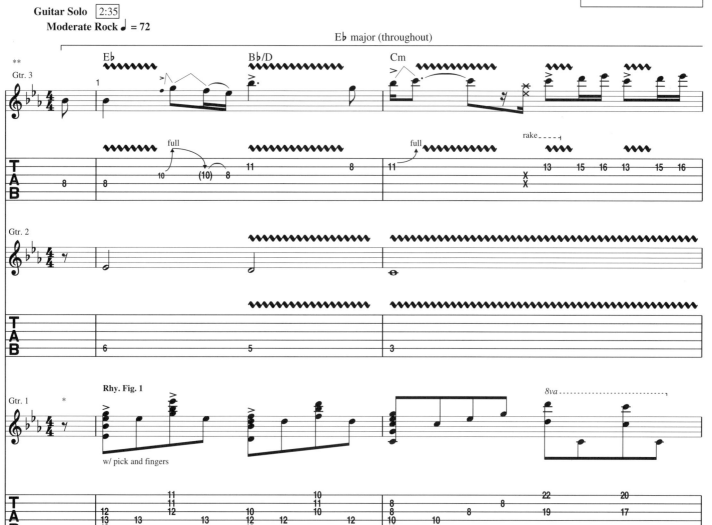

*piano arr. for gtr.

**Audio begins 6 meas. before Fig. 12

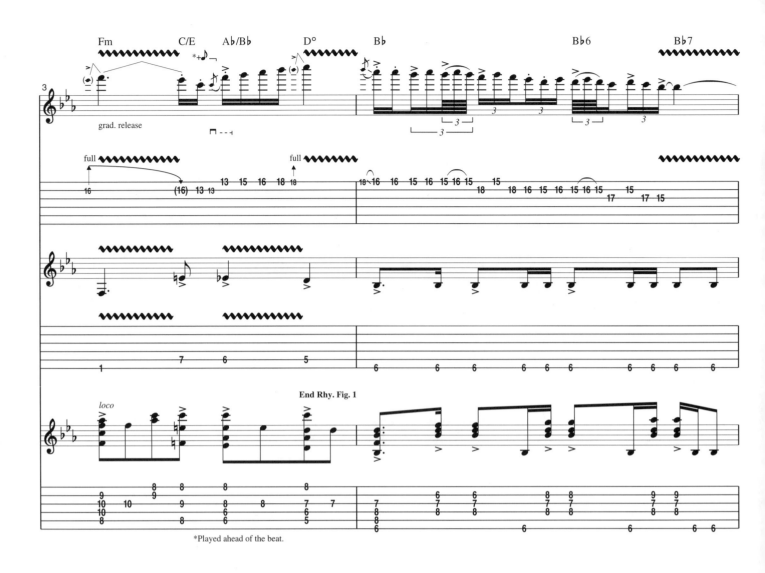

*Played ahead of the beat.

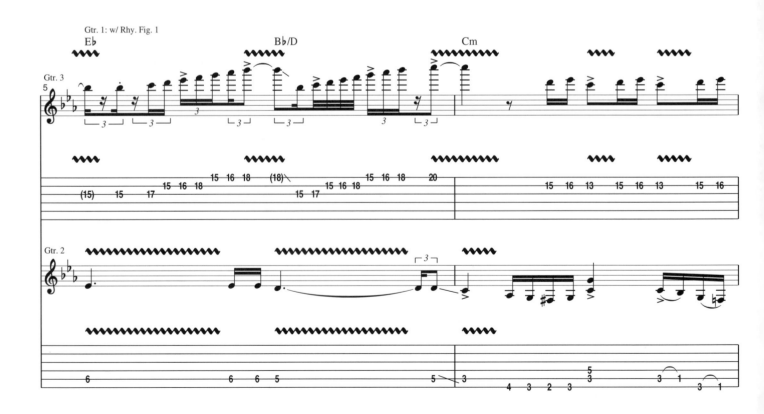

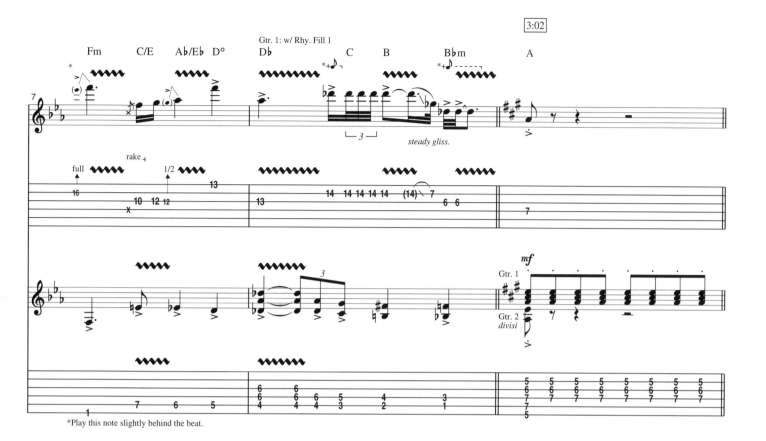

*Play this note slightly behind the beat.

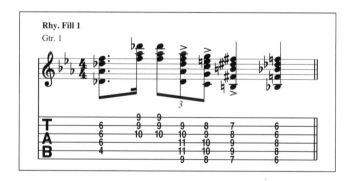

WALK THIS WAY
Words and Music by Steven Tyler and Joe Perry

Figure 1 – Second Guitar Solo and Outro Guitar Solo

Aerosmith struck twice with this powerful, guitar-driven classic: first in 1976 (#1) and a second time when guesting on the cover version with rappers Run-D.M.C. (#4, August, 1986). The defining track from Aerosmith's masterful *Toys in the Attic* album, "Walk This Way" personified the best of American hard rock in the seventies, and remains a favorite on everybody's classic rock playlist. Sporting an ultra-funky main guitar riff and an inspired set of Steven Tyler lyrics, it is further distinguished by some rock-solid Joe Perry soloing. A song high point is the multi-sectional Perry guitar solo in the outro.

This immortal Aerosmith solo is one of Joe Perry's milestone moments of the seventies, and can be divided into three sections. The first is the four-measure guitar episode in C, which is a second pass on the song's internal solo. It is played over the energetic verse groove. The eight-measure segue to E and into the outro solo represents the second section. The third section is the improvised outro solo which runs to the fade out. It's played in E over a variant of the song's funky main riff.

Scales used: Measures 1–4: C Mixolydian mode (C–D–E–F–G–A–B♭), C Dorian mode (C–D–E♭–F–G–A–B♭); measures 5–28: E Dorian mode (E–F♯–G–A–B–C♯–D), E Blues Scale (E–G–A–B♭–B–D), E Mixolydian mode (E–F♯–G♯–A–B–C♯–D), E minor pentatonic (E–G–A–B–D).

Significant added tones: E♭ (measure 1); E (measures 3–4); B♭ (measure 26)

Solo signatures: Free use of scales and scale combining; typically unpredictable Joe Perry rock 'n' roll phrasing; blues-rock oriented string bending and vibrato; prevalent use of hammer-ons and pull-offs.

Performance notes: The opening four measures are situated in the eighth and fifth positions and mix C dominant seventh and minor sounds in C. This is emphasized by the outlining of a C7 arpeggio in measure 2. The whammy bar is used for vibrato in the riffs of measures 5–12. These are thematic figures in E which are played in the second and twelfth positions. The bulk of the outro solo (measures 13–28) is played predominately in the twelfth position, and alternates with first position open-string licks in measures 21–26. A chords are inserted into the lead parts in measures 14, 16, 22, 24, and 26. These play off the accents of the background riff.

Sound: Gibson Les Paul and Fender Stratocaster; Marshall or Fender amps; delay (tight reflection) probably added to the outro guitar sound in the studio.

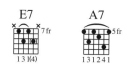

Fig. 1

Guitar Solo
Moderate Rock ♩ = 120

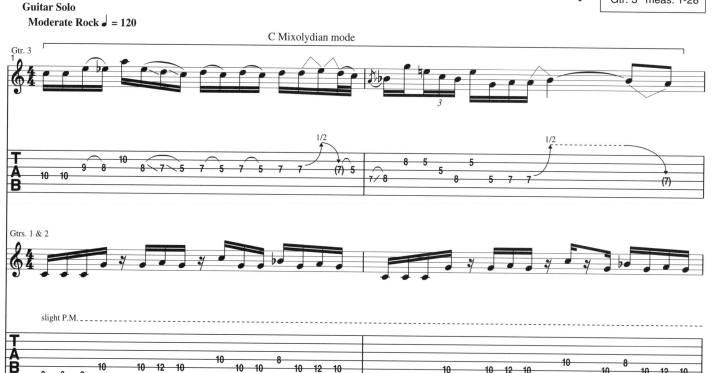

Outro Guitar Solo

Gtrs. 1 & 2: w/ Riff B, till fade

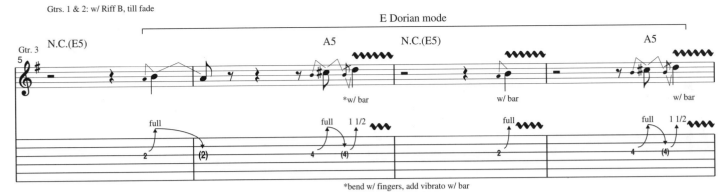

*bend w/ fingers, add vibrato w/ bar

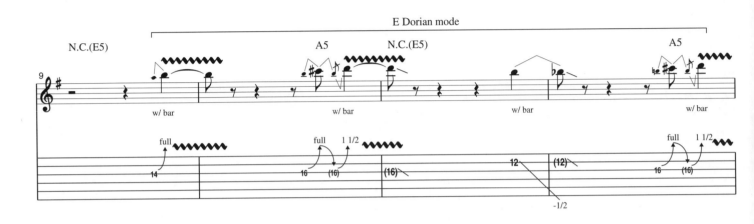

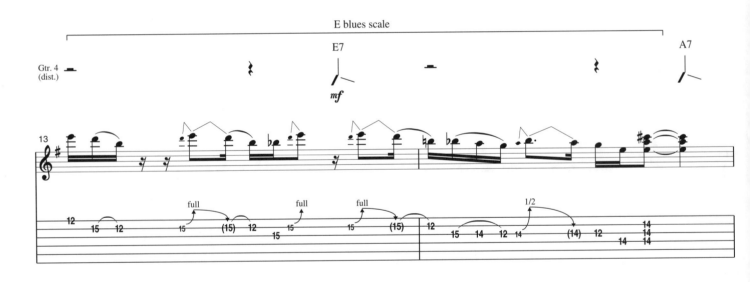

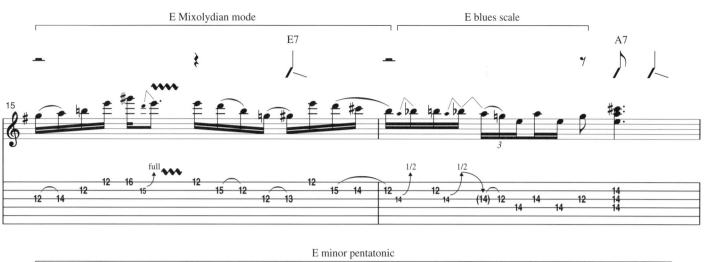

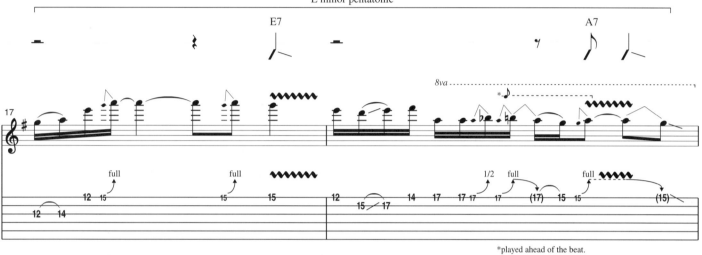

*played ahead of the beat.

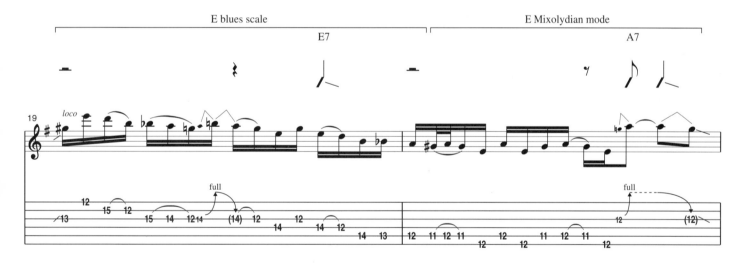

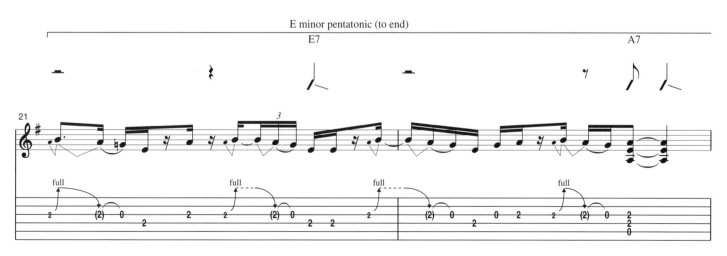

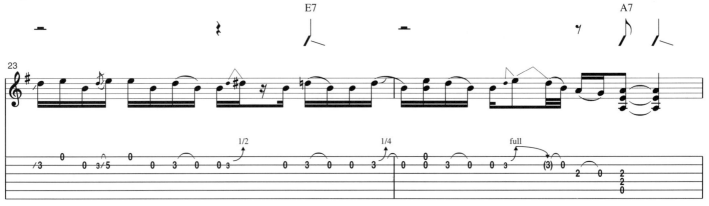

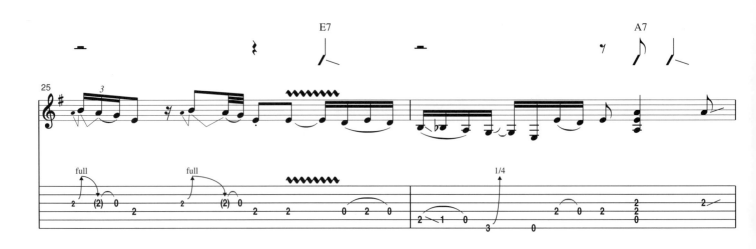

Fade Out

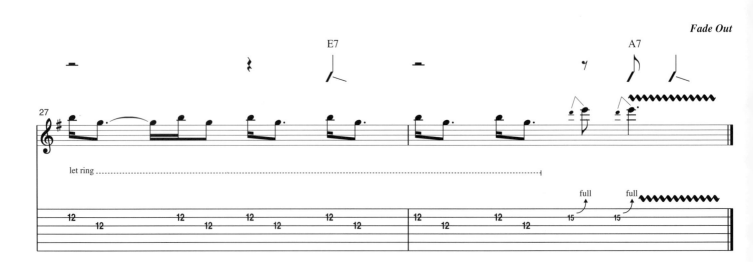

SULTANS OF SWING

Words and Music by Mark Knopfler

Figure 1 – Outro Guitar Solo

"Sultans of Swing" was Dire Straits' first hit. Seeming to emerge from out of nowhere, the unorthodox British rock band exploded onto the pop scene with the tremendous 1977 single, and a compelling debut album (*Dire Straits*). "Sultans of Swing" also introduced the "alternative" approach of lead guitarist Mark Knopfler. Unique among rock guitarists of the day, Knopfler eschewed the crunchy Marshall distortion and heavy metal-based approach of his fellow British fretmen, and fashioned his signature sound from a combination of esoteric melodic ideas delivered with a sparkling clean tone. Noted for exerting an enormous influence in the future, on both sides of the Atlantic, Knopfler's inimitable finger-style articulation, coupled with his distinctive Strat timbre, was immediately acknowledged and revered as the "Mark Knopfler sound."

No tune provides a better showcase than "Sultans of Swing" and no section more ably demonstrates his uncommon solo style than its extraordinary outro (4:58 to the fade out). The solo occurs over a four-measure vamp of the modal changes Dm–C–B♭–C, and skillfully balances impressive physical technique and song-conscious feel.

Scales used: D minor pentatonic (D–F–G–A–C); C major pentatonic (C–D–E–G–A); C Mixolydian mode (C–D–E–F–G–A–B♭).

Significant added tones: B♭ (measure 11)—though part of the C Mixolydian mode, the use of B♭ in this line is so melodically striking that it's particularly worth noting.

Solo signatures: Use of arpeggios, diatonic and pentatonic melody; pedal steel-style string bends; ostinato riffs (measures 7–8); melodic sequences (measures 3–4 and 20–21); virtual absence of standard rock guitar clichés.

Performance notes: This signature, predominately single-note Mark Knopfler solo is played fingerstyle on electric guitar. In addition to his very personalized plucked/picked attack, Knopfler favors the "in-between tone" of a Fender Strat—which adds much to the overall character of the guitar sound and his solo lines. The famed cascade of sixteenth-note arpeggios in measures 13–17 has become a hallmark of his style. This passage requires considerable dexterity to pull off at tempo. One of the keys to mastering this phrase is to visualize the three physical shapes of the Dm, B♭ and C arpeggios which comprise the section, and to note the commonalities. Notice that all three are situated on the top two strings, and are constructed of two notes on the first string (which are played legato with a pull-off) and one on the second string. This pattern is continued through the eight-measure phrase, though subtly altered to fit the changing chord progression.

Sound: Fender Stratocaster; Fender Vibrolux amp; delay—either via an MXR Analog Delay or added in the studio.

Fig. 1

Outro Guitar Solo 4:58

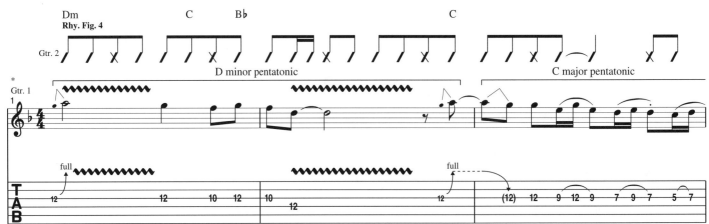

*Audio begins 8 meas. before Fig. 14

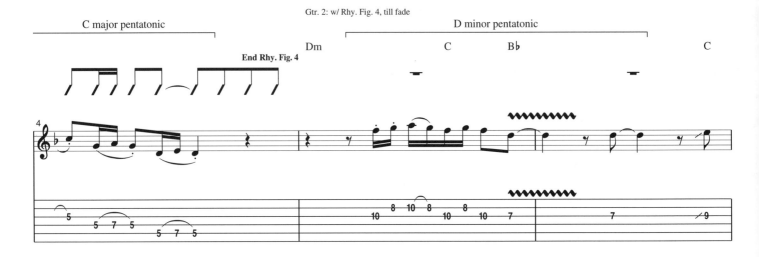

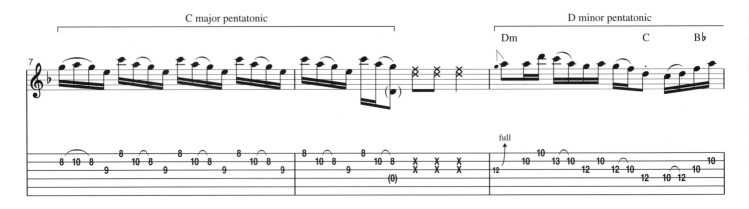

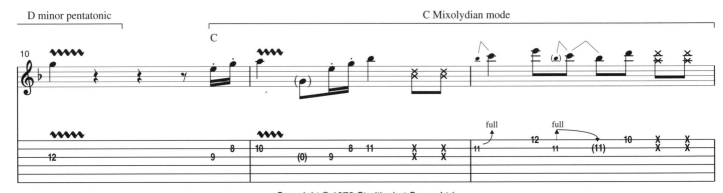

56

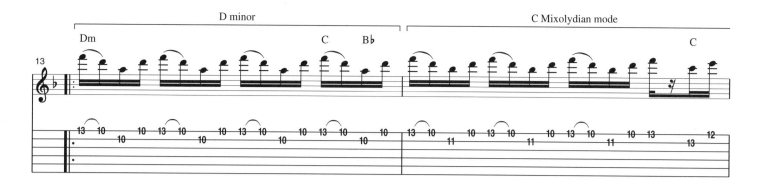

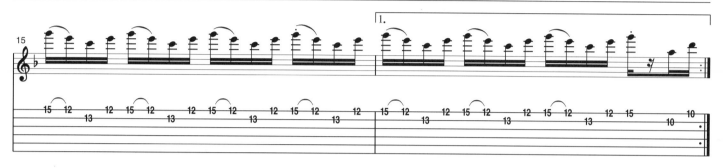

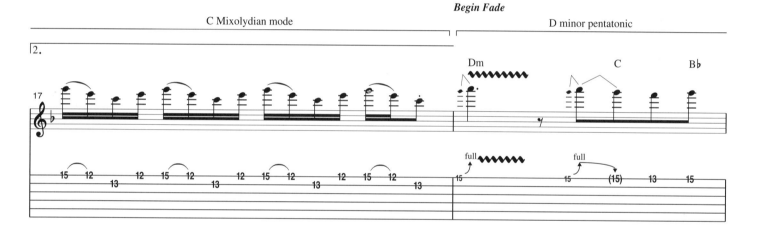

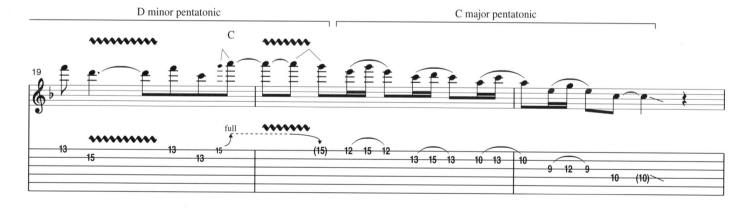

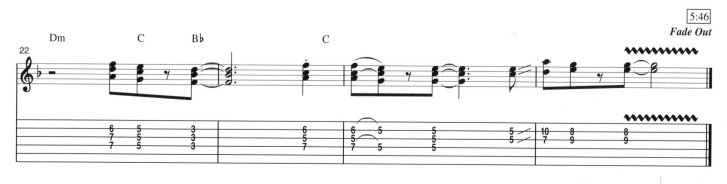

YOU REALLY GOT ME

Words and Music by Ray Davies

Figure 1 – Guitar Solo

Modern rock guitar was born on this 1978 remake of the Kinks' classic tune. Eddie Van Halen and company turned the already-driving, mid-sixties number into "a jet airplane" on the debut album, and produced one of the most momentous paradigm shifts in rock guitar music. Eddie pioneered many of the modern "shred" techniques, which would prove so dominant in the next decade, on the early Van Halen albums—particularly the groundbreaking first record, *Van Halen*. Today his legacy is assured. He is universally acknowledged as the most innovative and stunning player since Jimi Hendrix, and has generated a sphere of influence accorded to only a select handful of guitar players in history.

"You Really Got Me," a prominent cut from *Van Halen,* was an early Van Halen hit which introduced several of Ed's blazing signature licks to a grateful musical world. Eddie's brief but event-filled solo takes place over a simple vamp on A. It contains many of the trademark elements of his influential guitar style and, for most musicians, auspiciously marks the birth of "shred."

Scales used: A minor pentatonic (A–C–D–E–G); A major pentatonic (A–B–C♯–E–F♯).

Significant added tones: E♭, F, and F♯ (measure 4); B (measure 6), as a result of extreme string bends; G (measure 7–8); C and D (measure 9).

Solo signatures: Free mixture of minor and major pentatonic scales; tap-on technique; string bending with tap-on technique; extreme string bending (major third and fourth intervals!); standard rock guitar cliches mixed with mind-boggling guitar "tricks."

Performance notes: The tap-on licks in measures 3–5 are now synonymous with Van Halen's lead style. Eddie plays these tap-ons with his right-hand index finger, combining normal fretted notes with the higher tapped notes. Eddie silences any unwanted notes with fret-hand muting. In measure 4, the tap-on technique is used to create a descending, triplet-arpeggio effect with the higher tapped note functioning as a static pedal tone. In measure 5, the high G note is produced by bending the G string one whole step and fretting the tenth fret with tap-on technique. The wide string bending in measures 6–8 includes minor and major thirds, and a perfect fourth. That's five frets distance! The "helicopter" tremolo noise in measures 11–13 is generated by setting the neck pickup volume to 0 and the bridge pickup to 10, and flicking the pickup selector toggle switch in a specific rhythm. Eddie tunes all six strings down one half step (E flat tuning).

Sound: Ibanez Destroyer (copy of Gibson Explorer) with two humbucking pickups; overdriven late-60s "Plexi" Marshall 100-watt Super Lead amp; voltage altered with an Ohmite Variac; homemade pedalboard fitted with MXR Flanger, MXR Phase 90, Maestro echoplex.

Before playing along with Fig. 1, tune down one half step with track 31.

Fig. 1

Tune Down 1/2 Step:
① = E♭ ④ = D♭
② = B♭ ⑤ = A♭
③ = G♭ ⑥ = E♭

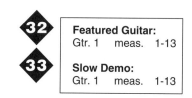

Featured Guitar:
Gtr. 1   meas.   1-13

Slow Demo:
Gtr. 1   meas.   1-13

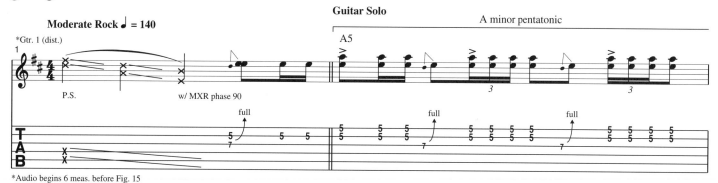

Moderate Rock ♩ = 140

Guitar Solo

A minor pentatonic

*Gtr. 1 (dist.)

P.S.   w/ MXR phase 90

*Audio begins 6 meas. before Fig. 15

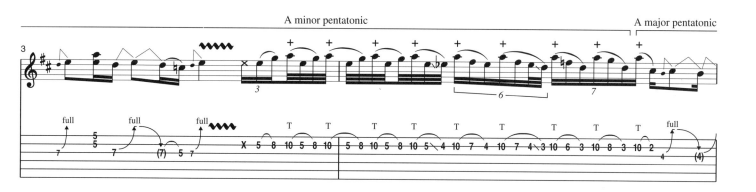

A minor pentatonic   A major pentatonic

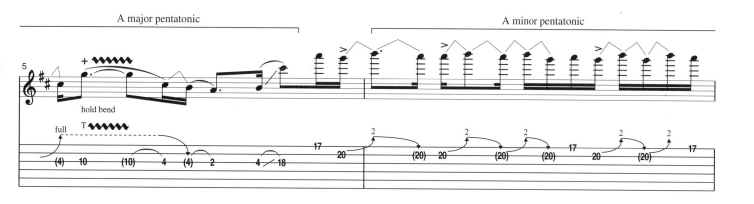

A major pentatonic   A minor pentatonic

hold bend

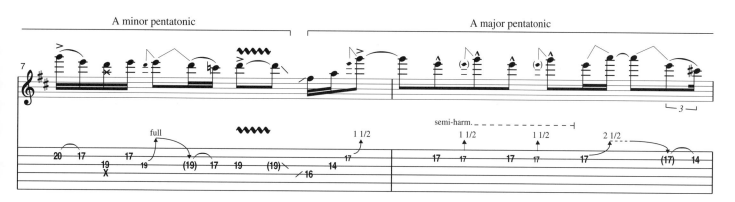

A minor pentatonic   A major pentatonic

semi-harm.

A major pentatonic

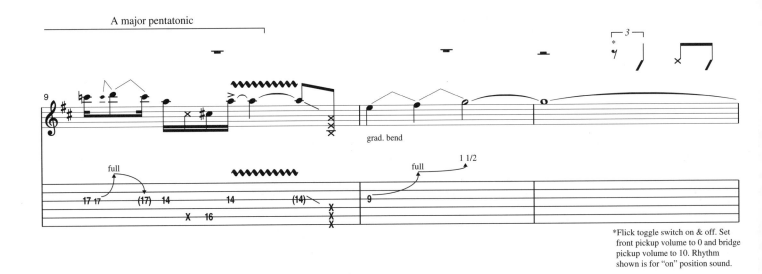

grad. bend

*Flick toggle switch on & off. Set
front pickup volume to 0 and bridge
pickup volume to 10. Rhythm
shown is for "on" position sound.

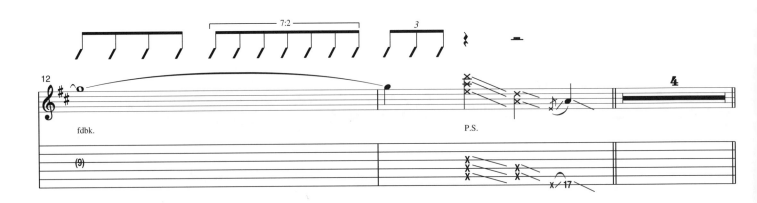

fdbk.

P.S.

CRAZY TRAIN

Words and Music by Ozzy Osbourne, Randy Rhoads, and Bob Daisley

Figure 1 – Guitar Solo

If "shred" was introduced with the first Van Halen record, then the ante was upped to higher stakes on the milestone Ozzy Osbourne release of 1981, *The Blizzard of Ozz.* Randy Rhoads, lead guitarist and collaborator with Ozzy, epitomized the modern metal genre which was all-pervasive in the eighties, and defined dramatic new standards for guitar orchestration and technique. Though similar to Van Halen's playing in several superficial aspects, Randy's style was a striking departure from the more straightahead, hard rock/blues-based jamming antics of Eddie and the legions of L.A. guitar clones he had engendered. By contrast, Randy favored a thoughtful "neo-classic" approach in which his guitar solos were crafted as strong, often independent, musical interludes—compositions within compositions—for more complicated works. Fretboard virtuosity nicknamed "shred" still prevailed in the Ozzy material, but it had a substantially different setting, characterized by minor tonality, exotic scale choices, and larger-scale form.

"Crazy Train" is perhaps the most visible Randy Rhoads offering of his brief career. The song combines the power and crunch of heavy metal with the pronounced melodic sensibilities of classical music and the florid passagework of the shred school. Randy's dazzling signature solo in "Crazy Train" occurs over sixteen measures of modal chord changes in F♯ minor.

Scales used: F♯ natural minor or Aeolian mode (F♯–G♯–A–B–C♯–D–E).

Significant added tones: D♯ (measure 15).

Solo signatures: Semi-classical metal approach emphasizing minor modality, baroque/classical melody, and integrated virtuosity; legato technique (abundant use of hammer-ons and pull-offs); sectional thematic structure with a strong climax.

Performance notes: The solo is well constructed with logical question-and-answer phrases, generally arranged in four-measure sections. Tap-on technique is used in measures 1–4. This produces F♯ minor and D major arpeggios in measures 1 and 2. Tap-on technique is combined with string bending and releasing in measure 3. The legato phrases in measures 7 and 15 are Randy Rhoads signature licks. The latter is played by hammering on groups of three-note-per-string scale patterns. Randy uses the technique to create an ascending climactic run. The entire solo is doubled by a second lead guitar which accounts for the thick chorused sound.

Sound: Gibson Les Paul Custom; overdriven Marshall 100-watt stack; MXR Distortion Plus.

Fig. 1

Guitar Solo
Moderate Rock ♩ = 138

*Audio begins 8 meas. before Fig. 1
**Gtr. solo doubled. Slight discrepancies between two gtrs. result in heavily chorused effect.

* This measure played simile on demo
** Played ahead of the beat

* Next 2 meas. played simile on demo.

CROSSFIRE

Written by Bill Carter, Ruth Ellsworth, Chris Layton, Tommy Shannon, and Reese Wynans

Figure 1 – Guitar Solo

Stevie Ray Vaughan reignited the blues fire in the early eighties. By decade's end, he had attained mythic proportions and was the leading force in the genre. Stevie was a genuine bluesman straight out of the tradition. His guitar influences (he called them his "books") included B.B. and Albert King, Buddy Guy, Eric Clapton, Lonnie Mack, and Jimi Hendrix. He absorbed all their lessons and then some. His self-professed goal was to "take the color out of the blues." By the time of his death in 1990, he had accomplished that mission decisively. *In Step* (1989) marked a milestone for Stevie—presenting him and Double Trouble as recording artists as well as the country's top blues trio. The album went gold in the first six months, won a Grammy for Best Contemporary Blues Recording, and also won Austin Music Awards' Record of the Year and Single of the Year, "Crossfire."

"Crossfire," a funky R&B/rock number, has since endured to become a gigantic album rock hit and represents some of Vaughan's finest playing ever. Stevie's primary solo in "Crossfire" is twenty-four measures long. It takes place over a heavy, Stax-inspired vamp in E, based on a riff rather than a 12-bar blues, during the first sixteen measures. In measures 17–24, Stevie plays over the bridge changes: G7–A7–G7–A7–E.

Scales used: E minor pentatonic (E–G–A–B–D).

Significant added tones: G♯, B♭—almost all as a result of string bending; C♯ (measure 23).

Solo signatures: Blues phrasing and melodies in a rock/R&B context; Stevie's favored "Albert King lick" throughout (indicated by small brackets); Stevie Ray Vaughan tuned all six strings down one half step (E flat tuning).

Performance notes: This unforgettable SRV solo is played in the primary blues-box in E at the the twelfth position and the "Albert box" at the fifteenth position. The emphasis is on traditional electric blues melody with string bending and finger vibrato. To perform the bends with the same fluidity (especially with heavy strings), use reinforced fingering to push the strings with more than one fretting finger. The two-string bends in measure 13 are signatures of Stevie's lead style. These are played by hooking two strings at a time, in this case the high E and B, under the fretting finger(s), and bending both.

Sound: Fender Stratocaster with heavy-gauge strings; various amps used during the *In Step* sessions included Fender Super Reverbs and Vibroverbs, a Fender tweed '59 Bassman and '62 Twin, Marshall JCM 800 and 200-watt heads into 4x15 and 8x10 cabinets; Ibanez Tube Screamer.

Before playing along with Fig. 1, tune down one half step with track 31.

Fig. 1

Tune Down 1/2 Step:
① = Eb ④ = Db
② = Bb ⑤ = Ab
③ = Gb ⑥ = Eb

Guitar Solo 1:58

Moderate Rock ♩ = 116

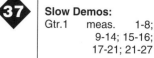

Featured Guitar:
Gtr.1 meas. 1-24

Slow Demos:
Gtr.1 meas. 1-8;
         9-14; 15-16;
         17-21; 21-27

E minor pentatonic throughout

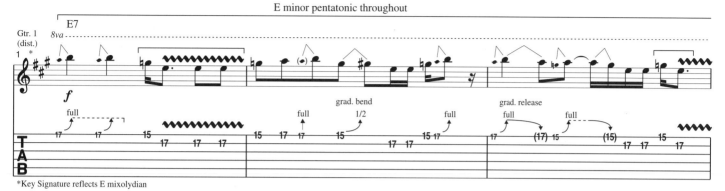

*Key Signature reflects E mixolydian

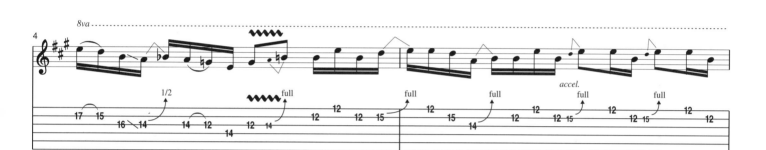

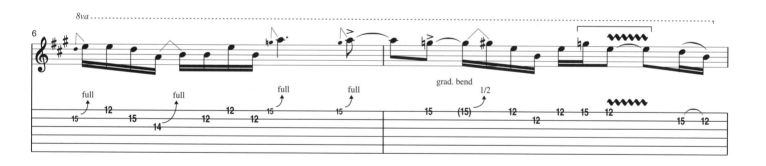

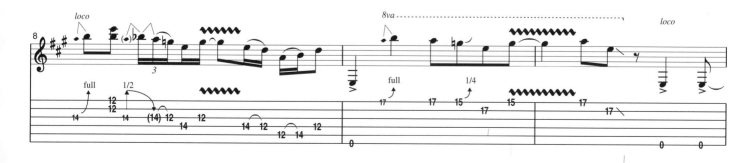

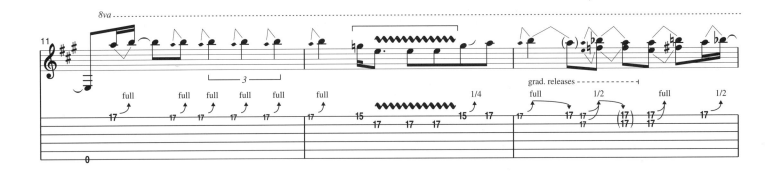

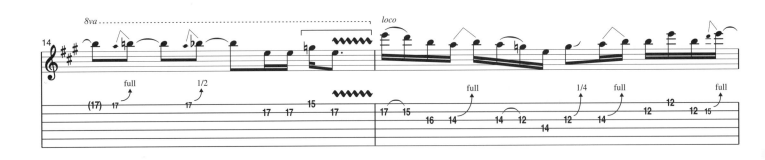

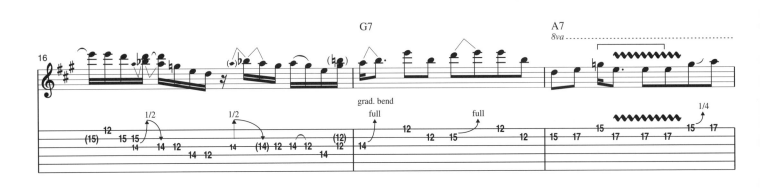

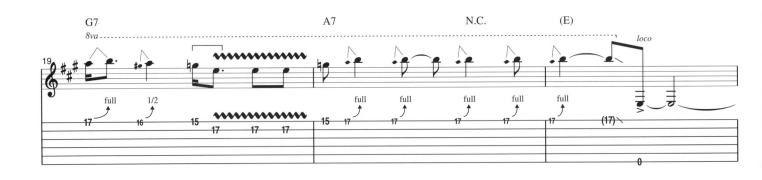

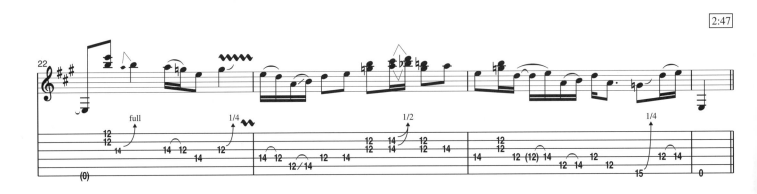

SWEET CHILD O' MINE

Words and Music by W. Axl Rose, Slash, Izzy Stradlin', Duff McKagan, and Steven Adler

Figure 1 – Guitar Solo

Slash came to the forefront in the late 1980s with the iconoclastic rock and punk group Guns N' Roses. In contrast with the over-produced pop metal and glam rock stars of the era, the Gunners were a tough, no-nonsense act—adopting and flaunting a decidedly "street" image and stripped-down sound. Ideally suited for the situation, Slash pioneered and popularized a "new retro" guitar style with strong implications for the nineties. His approach, with its roots in sixties blues-based hard rock and seventies metal, fit the GNR material perfectly and was a large factor in the success of the band.

"Sweet Child O' Mine," from the 1987 Guns N' Roses debut album *Appetite for Destruction,* is a milestone song for the band, and a career-defining moment for Slash as a guitarist. The track—one of their longest—was a colossal hit record, an MTV standard, and a perennial in-concert favorite, containing the quintessential Slash solo.

Scales used: E harmonic minor (E–F♯–G–A–B–C–D♯); E natural minor or Aeolian mode (E–F♯–G–A–B–C–D); E minor pentatonic (E–G–A–B–D).

Significant added tones: D♯ (measure 17); F♯ (measure 20–21) and B♭ (measure 23), as a result of string bends; F♯ (measure 29).

Solo signatures: Two-part sectional structure with a song-oriented balance of minor mode melody and blues licks; oblique string bends (measures 24–25); sequences (measures 28–29); ostinato riffs (measures 30–31); Slash tunes all six strings down one half step (E♭ tuning).

Performance notes: This landmark Slash solo is arranged in two sections with contrasting moods. The first is modal, and exploits chord progressions and diatonic melodies based on E minor. The second has a more driving hard rock feel with a simpler power-chord vamp of E–G–A–C–D–G, and is characterized by aggressive blues licks and string bends. The long, ascending harmonic minor scale run in measures 16 and 17 connects the two sections, and reflects the eighties "shred guitar" approach. Slash uses a wah-wah pedal during the second solo section. This is rocked in time with the phrasing of specific licks for a talking wah effect.

Sound: Gibson Les Paul Standard; 100-watt Marshall stack; wah-wah pedal.

Before playing along with Fig. 1, tune down one half step with track 31.

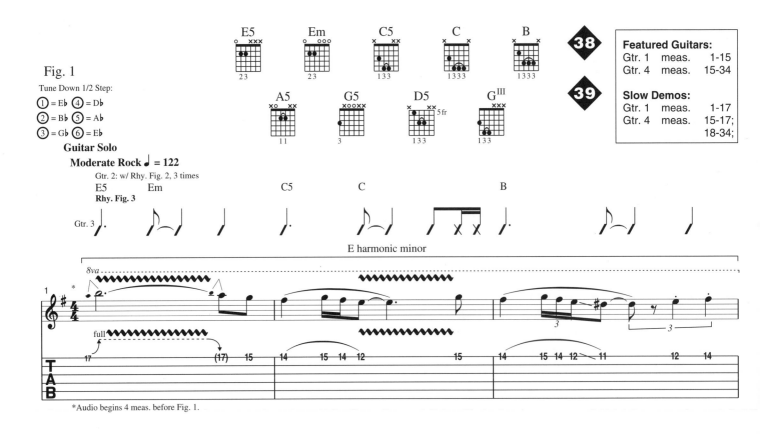

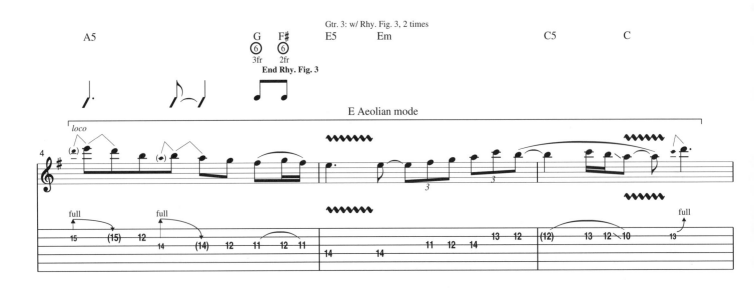

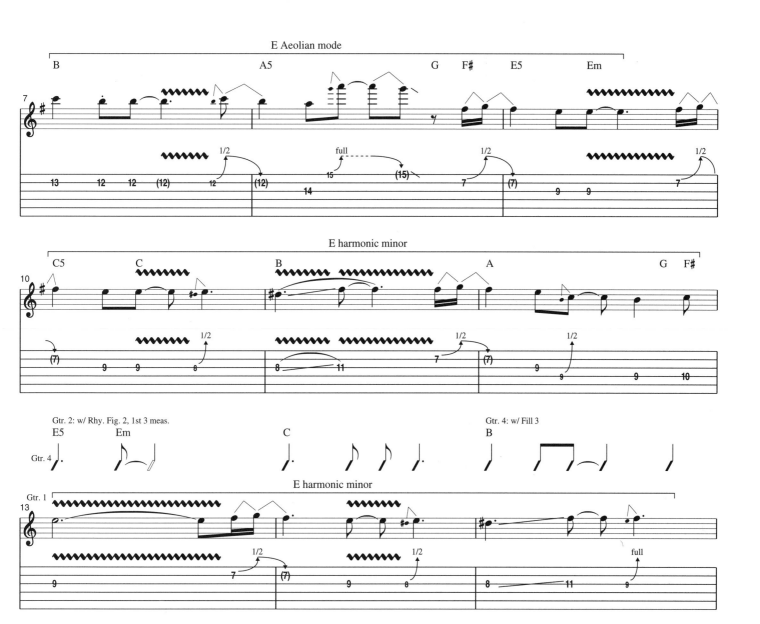

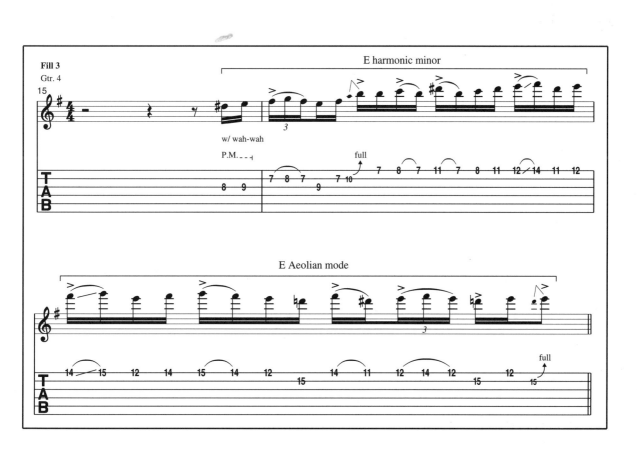

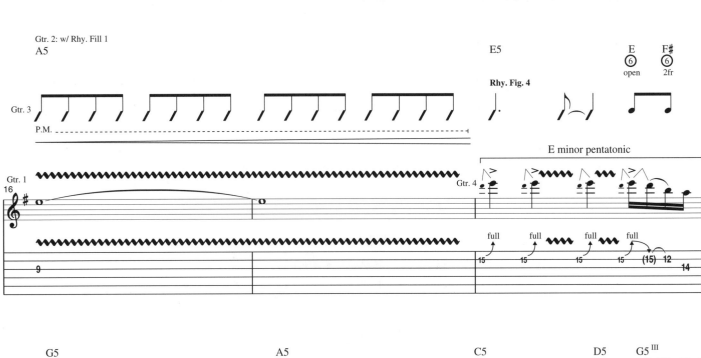

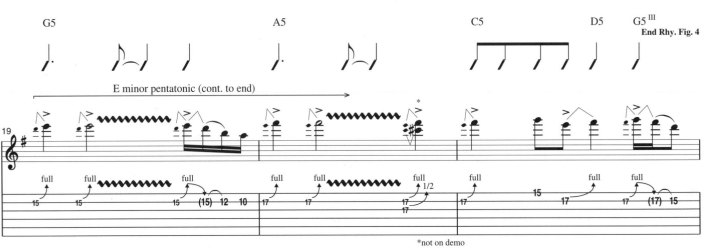

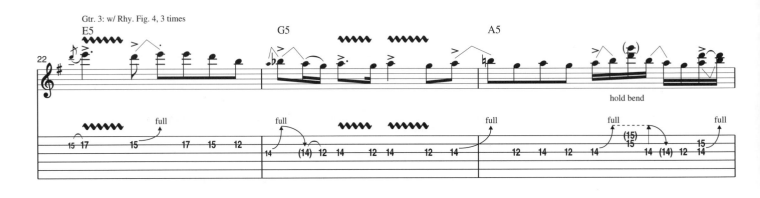

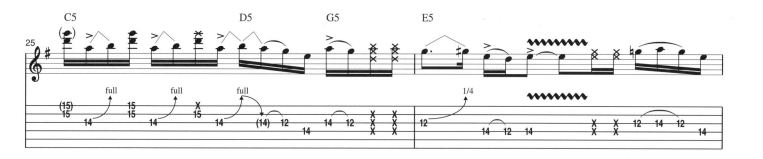

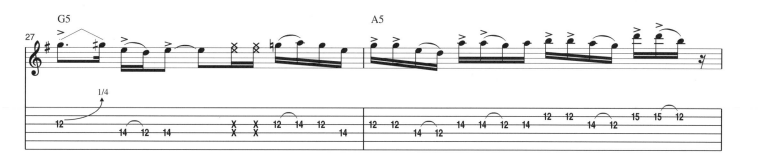

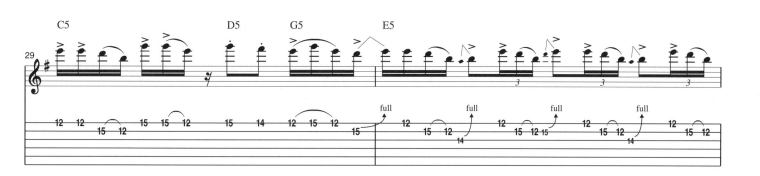

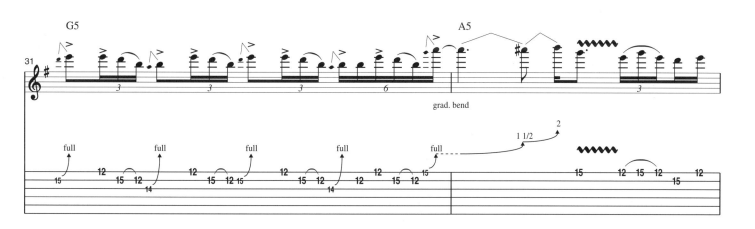

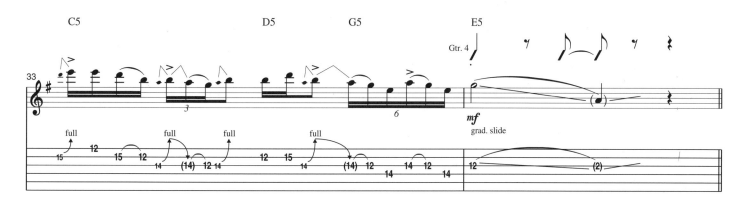

GUITAR NOTATION LEGEND

Guitar Music can be notated three different ways: on a *musical staff*, in *tablature*, and in *rhythm slashes*.

RHYTHM SLASHES are written above the staff. Strum chords in the rhythm indicated. Use the chord diagrams found at the top of the first page of the transcription for the appropriate chord voicings. Round noteheads indicate single notes.

THE MUSICAL STAFF shows pitches and rhythms and is divided by bar lines into measures. Pitches are named after the first seven letters of the alphabet.

TABLATURE graphically represents the guitar fingerboard. Each horizontal line represents a string, and each number represents a fret.

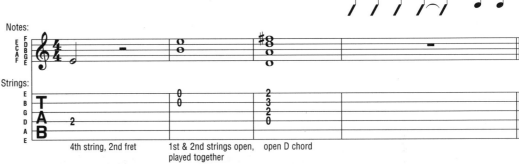

4th string, 2nd fret · 1st & 2nd strings open, played together · open D chord

---

HALF-STEP BEND: Strike the note and bend up 1/2 step.

WHOLE-STEP BEND: Strike the note and bend up one step.

GRACE NOTE BEND: Strike the note and bend up as indicated. The first note does not take up any time.

SLIGHT (MICROTONE) BEND: Strike the note and bend up 1/4 step.

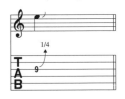

BEND AND RELEASE: Strike the note and bend up as indicated, then release back to the original note. Only the first note is struck.

PRE-BEND: Bend the note as indicated, then strike it.

VIBRATO: The string is vibrated by rapidly bending and releasing the note with the fretting hand.

WIDE VIBRATO: The pitch is varied to a greater degree by vibrating with the fretting hand.

HAMMER-ON: Strike the first (lower) note with one finger, then sound the higher note (on the same string) with another finger by fretting it without picking.

PULL-OFF: Place both fingers on the notes to be sounded. Strike the first note and without picking, pull the finger off to sound the second (lower) note.

LEGATO SLIDE: Strike the first note and then slide the same fret-hand finger up or down to the second note. The second note is not struck.

SHIFT SLIDE: Same as legato slide, except the second note is struck.

TRILL: Very rapidly alternate between the notes indicated by continuously hammering on and pulling off.

TAPPING: Hammer ("tap") the fret indicated with the pick-hand index or middle finger and pull off to the note fretted by the fret hand.

NATURAL HARMONIC: Strike the note while the fret-hand lightly touches the string directly over the fret indicated.

PINCH HARMONIC: The note is fretted normally and a harmonic is produced by adding the edge of the thumb or the tip of the index finger of the pick hand to the normal pick attack.

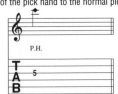

PICK SCRAPE: The edge of the pick is rubbed down (or up) the string, producing a scratchy sound.

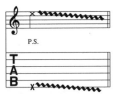

MUFFLED STRINGS: A percussive sound is produced by laying the fret hand across the string(s) without depressing, and striking them with the pick hand.

PALM MUTING: The note is partially muted by the pick hand lightly touching the string(s) just before the bridge.

RAKE: Drag the pick across the strings indicated with a single motion.

TREMOLO PICKING: The note is picked as rapidly and continuously as possible.

VIBRATO BAR DIVE AND RETURN: The pitch of the note or chord is dropped a specified number of steps (in rhythm) then returned to the original pitch.

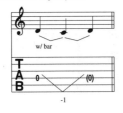

VIBRATO BAR SCOOP: Depress the bar just before striking the note, then quickly release the bar.

VIBRATO BAR DIP: Strike the note and then immediately drop a specified number of steps, then release back to the original pitch.